HOW TO STU

In this Series

other titles in preparation

STUDY ABROAD

Teresa Tinsley

Northcote House

First published in 1990 by Northcote House Publishers Ltd,
Plymbridge House, Estover Road, Plymouth PL6 7PZ,
United Kingdom. Tel: Plymouth (0752) 705251. Telex: 45635.
Fax: (0752) 777603.

British Library Cataloguing in Publication Data

Tinsley, Teresa, 1957-
  How to study abroad. — (How to books)
  1. Higher education institutions. Students. Overseas study
  I. Title
  378'.35

ISBN 0-7463-0340-8

Typeset by Cheshire Typesetters
Printed in Great Britain by BPCC Wheatons Ltd, Exeter

Contents

Key to Languages

The languages shown are those most commonly used in further education in each country.

English

Antigua
Australia
Bahamas
Bangladesh
Barbados
Belize
Botswana
Canada
Cyprus
Dominica
Eastern Caribbean States
Fiji
Gambia
Ghana
Grenada
Guyana
Hong Kong
India
Ireland
Israel
Jamaica
Kenya
Lesotho
Liberia
Malawi
Malaysia
Malta
Mauritius
New Zealand
Nigeria
Papua New Guinea
Philippines

Seychelles
Sierra Leone
Singapore
Solomon Islands
South Africa
Swaziland
Tanzania
Tonga
Trinidad and Tobago
Uganda
USA
Zambia
Zimbabwe

French

Algeria
Belgium
Benin
Burkina Faso
Burundi
Cameroon
Canada
Central African Republic
Chad
Congo
Cote d'Ivoire
France
Gabon
Guinea
Haiti
Luxembourg
Madagascar

Mali
Mauritania
Mauritius
Niger
Rwanda
Senegal
Switzerland
Togo
Tunisia
Vietnam
Zaire

Spanish

Argentina
Bolivia
Chile
Colombia
Costa Rica
Cuba
Ecuador
El Salvador
Honduras
Mexico
Nicaragua
Panama
Paraguay
Peru
Philippines
Spain
Uruguay
Venezuela

Preface

It is perhaps a truism to say that our world is getting smaller; but so much of our business is now conducted on the world stage that we are all being affected as never before by events beyond our shores. As Europe becomes a single market, as more and more businesses become multinational or at least depend on external markets, and as our contacts with the rest of the world develop along with modern communications, so we are increasingly being asked to consider our future in international terms. We can be sure that, for all sorts of people in many walks of life, the future will demand ever more knowledge and understanding of the way other countries do things. Knowledge of languages too will surely pass from being merely useful to becoming a vital tool for participation in this international future. One of the best ways of gaining this knowledge is a period of study abroad; only through familiarity with the language and the education system, and by living in the country, can we gain a better understanding of how people think and live abroad.

In centuries past it was the custom for a privileged minority to complete their education by making a Grand Tour of Europe and beyond. Since then we have seen a progressive democratisation of so many forms of educational opportunity that perhaps by the next century a period of study abroad will have become a normal part of many people's education.

This book is aimed, then, at this new generation of Western reader, whose reasons for wanting to study abroad (whether to broaden horizons or to improve prospects) reflect much greater individual aspiration. The tempting range of study possibilities, both in the West and further afield, can amply satisfy these objectives. However it's important to bear in mind that countries outside the Western world may have ideas about education which are less individualistic. For example in Islamic countries education has a social role tightly bound up with religion; in Eastern Europe it has traditionally been economic needs which have determined the education available. Education has a different role to play in countries which have different educational traditions, which are at a different stage of development, or where the educational system has evolved in a different way. Even within the West education systems vary enormously, as do people's expectations of them. It is not possible to stick a pin in a map of the world and expect to be able to import all our own preconceived ideas about education. This is especially important in the case of developing countries, where for many people even basic education may not be readily available. So, while it is hoped this book will encourage you to study abroad, and to show you how, do consider not only what the country can give you, but what you can bring to it. Good luck!

Publishers' note

Whilst every effort has been made to ensure the accuracy of the information given in this book, contact addresses are liable to change and study conditions may vary, especially in countries subject to political upheaval.

As this book was going to press, the STD code for London phone numbers changed from 01 to 071 for inner London and 081 for outer London.

1
Why Study Abroad?

THE ATTRACTIONS

What is attractive about studying abroad when so many educational
opportunities exist in our own country? Is it the excitement and
challenge of the chance to spend some time in a foreign country,
or the lure of courses and qualifications which aren't available here?

- There may be strong **personal reasons** why you feel attracted
  to a particular country — because you've already spent some
  time there, because you have friends or family there, or perhaps
  because you speak the language.

- You may be attracted to the possibility of obtaining different
  qualifications from those you can get at home, especially if you
  plan to live and work abroad afterwards.

- The experience of having lived and studied abroad may be
  valuable for your future **career** and can look impressive on a
  CV.

- If your interest is some **specialist subject** connected with a particular country or an area of the world (whether it's Inca archaeology or the life cycle of the Tibetan mountain rat) then
  obviously the subject is much better studied in situ: courses may
  simply not be available at home.

- If you haven't been able to get a **place** on a particular course
  of study in the UK, you may want to see whether other countries offer easier access. This is as valid a reason as any for wanting to study abroad, so there's no need to be ashamed about
  it! But try and be realistic about your own capabilities and limitations: are you really up to it? Is this course really you, or would

a different course altogether be more suitable?

- Finally, perhaps the most obvious reasons for wanting to study abroad are purely educational: to **broaden your horizons,** to make contact with another culture, to learn through the medium of another language. These are certainly excellent reasons. If you're going to do a first degree abroad, be especially prepared for the power the experience of living and studying abroad can have in shaping your future and outlook.

What are *your* reasons for studying abroad? If you are clear what you want out of the experience you will find it much easier to choose which country, which course, and which institution can offer you the best opportunity.

The drawbacks
There can of course be drawbacks to studying abroad:

- Application and admissions **procedures** can be much harder to cope with than in your own country (even with the aid of this guide!).

- **Information** about the course, accommodation, conditions and so on is sometimes difficult to check in advance.

- The **qualifications** you get may not be recognised in the UK on your return.

- If you are going to be abroad for some while, you may find it hard to pick up the threads of your life in the UK when you return: getting back into the job market, **re-establishing yourself.** . .

- Study abroad may involve more **expense,** not only in terms of fees but also living and travel costs.

- The **travel itself** may be an unwanted burden, especially if you are going a long way afield.

- Abandoning your **commitments** at home may be a problem, whether they be family or social. The idea of leaving good friends and having to make new ones in a strange environment is not always attractive.

Pros and cons of study abroad

Pros	*Cons*
Broadens horizons	Expensive (possibly)
Experience of a lifetime	Hard to leave friends/commitments at home
Study possibilities not available in the UK	Cumbersome arrangements
Qualifications not available in UK	Difficult to check out in advance
Experience looks good on CV	Qualifications may not be recognised
	Difficulties in re-establishing in UK on return

If the situations looks tilted towards the 'cons' at the moment, don't worry too much. This book will point out possible pitfalls, to help you avoid them. It will take you step by step through all the practical arrangements that need to be made, so that, whatever type of course you choose, your experience of studying abroad will have every chance of being both enjoyable and rewarding.

ARE YOU THE TYPE TO STUDY ABROAD?

If you've not spent time abroad before, you may wonder how you'll cope living and studying in a foreign country, especially if you're going to be away for some time. Are you cut out for it? What personal qualities help to make the experience a successful one?

Adaptability is vital: a willingness to accept other ways of life. It's being able to adapt to the little everyday routines — different food, times of meals and so forth, that really helps you to feel at home in a foreign country; if you can't exist without a cup of British tea every few hours, perhaps you'd better think again!

Tolerance: you don't have to adapt to *all* aspects of a country's way of life in order to survive there, but it does help to have a tolerant attitude towards any cultural or religious differences. Ask yourself how you react on holiday to other customs and ways of life. What indeed is your attitude to ethnic cultures in *this* country? If the 'foreign-ness' makes you laugh, remember the joke will be on you when you are abroad.

Independence. How do you feel about 'going it alone', away from family and friends? Do you relish the idea or are you worried about being a stranger in a foreign country?

Practicality. How practical are you, in the sense of being able to find your way around in new places? Have you got a good sense of direction? Do you easily cope with a new job, or in an unknown town or city? You can help yourself by keeping instructions, maps, timetables etc to hand at all times, and by studying them thoroughly.

Outgoing personality. Many of the initial difficulties of settling down in a new place can be overcome if you are sufficiently extrovert to ask questions, to make new contacts and new friends. How good are you at talking to strangers?

Languages. Depending on which country you're going to, a knowledge of a foreign language can be crucial. Do you have an ear for languages? Even if your present knowledge is limited, it can improve dramatically once you're in the country if you have an ability to pick up new words and phrases quickly.

Checklist

Is studying abroad practical for you?

Will the qualifications obtained be of real value to you?

Will the experience be recognised as valid by future employers?

Will it work out very expensive? Can you afford it?

Can you reasonably expect to get some help with funding? (see p.49)

Does the course merit the travel involved?

Do you need a visa/residence permit to travel to the country concerned?

Are these easily available? (see p.38)

THE COURSE FOR YOU

Study opportunities abroad are many and varied. This book will give you a taste of what is available and help you decide which course is for you. The opportunities available have had a big boost in recent years by the European Community's policy of encouraging students to spend some time studying in a country rather than their own, and the number of **Joint Study Programmes** (see p.21), is increasing every year. You can even do your whole degree in another European country, if your languages are up to it! See p.19 for further details. And on the subject of languages, these new study opportunities have given a new relevance to foreign language learning: the best place to learn a language is in the country concerned, so check out the range of public and private **language courses** in each country.

The European Community is not of course by any means the only option for study abroad. There are schemes which allow you to go on **work placements** in Scandinavia, spend a term at a school in the United States, take part in **development projects** in the Third World, or do research in a **Commonwealth country.** If you're working and haven't got much time to spare, international **summer schools** are held all over the world, for specialists and non-specialists alike. Then of course there are **international schools, colleges and universities** in many different parts of the world offering everything from Cordon Bleu Cookery to doctoral degrees.

Is the political situation in the country concerned reasonably stable? (You don't want to arrive to find universities closed, access to archives restricted and running battles on the street!)
Accommodation. Is the sort of accommodation you require readily available at a reasonable price?
Health and welfare. Do you have any special requirements in this area, for instance a special diet, childcare facilities? Will these needs be taken care of?
What sort of social provision exists to help you fit in well?

Should I study abroad? — the decision-making process

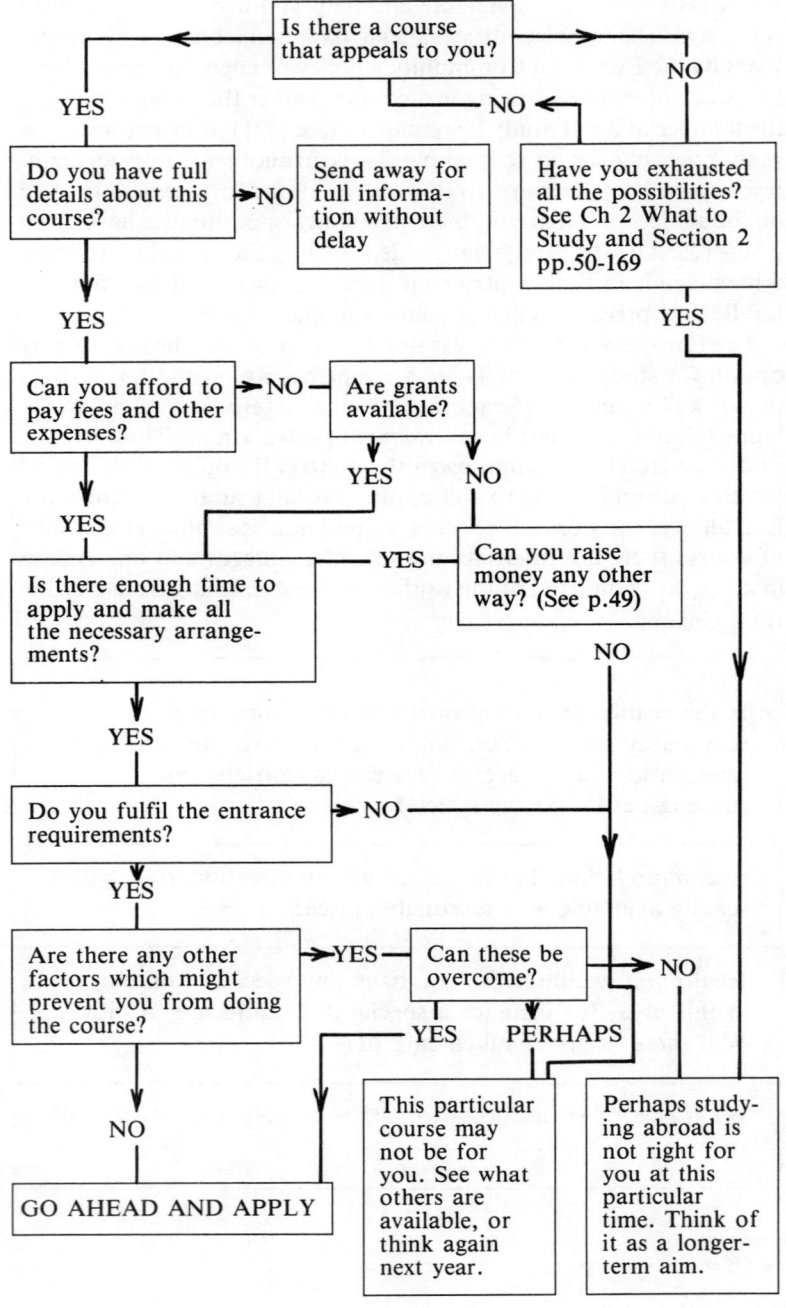

The next chapter will look in detail at these opportunities, and show you which courses are open to you. Section 2 of this book, which starts on p.50, will give you an idea of the possibilities in each country. To help you decide, p.6 shows a list of countries which use English, French or Spanish as a medium of instruction.

2
Study Opportunities Available

What sort of openings are available for *you?* These are likely to vary according to your age, experience and level of previous studies, so this chapter deals successively with opportunities for:

- 16-19 year olds
- undergraduates, both prospective and current
- postgraduates
- post experience and mature students.

Don't forget that not all options are available in every country, so refer also to Section 2 of this guide, which starts on p.50.

OPPORTUNITIES FOR YOUNG PEOPLE

The opportunities under this heading are likely to be of interest to you if you are still at school, if you've just left, or if you've only been in work or training for a short while.

School year abroad programmes

How about spending a term or a year abroad living with a foreign family and attending a local school? (though you shouldn't interrupt an A level course to do this). This is an especially good way of learning a foreign language, although you'll really need a good working knowledge before you go, just in order to survive! If you've already been on a **student exchange** to the country concerned, this is a good preparation. If it was successful and you can stay with the same family again, but this time attend school, so much the better! If you're not much good at languages you may feel you'd prefer to go for an English speaking country; this experience too can be very worthwhile.

How to arrange a year or a term abroad

It's perfectly possible to make such arrangements independently through personal contacts; provided you get all the details sorted out in advance, these can work very well. There's no one set formula, and the sort of arrangements you make will depend on personal preference, on the family concerned, and on other variables. The sort of points you will need to keep in mind are listed below.

If you have no personal contacts in the country concerned however, there are agencies which can make arrangements for you:

ASSE International School Year Abroad Programme, 6 Harcourt Street, London W1H 2BD, tel (01) 724 0280 (USA, Canada, Australia and New Zealand).

International Educational Programmes, Seymour Mews House, Seymour Mews, London W1H 9PE, tel (01) 486 5462 (Europe, Latin America, the Far East, Australia, Egypt).

For further information on homestays and exchanges, the Central Bureau's publication *Home from Home* is available (see p.171).

Checklist of points to remember:

The school
- Will you contact the school directly, or will the family do this for you?
- What sort of curriculum will you be studying?
- Are there any special arrangements for language lessons?
- Will the school make a charge? (Is it private or state-run?)
- How many hours per day/week will you spend in school?
- How far will you have to travel each day to get to school?

The Family
- Do they have children your age? (Ideally they should be attending the same school, so they can show you around and help you settle in.)
- Are they charging, or are they taking you on an exchange basis?
- If charging, what exactly does this include? (meals, transport, additional expenses, etc).

International schools

Theoretically any institution can call itself 'international', and so hope to attract students from other countries. Such institutions may include:

1. Schools in various countries which do not follow the education
    system of that country. Did you know for example that there
    are schools all over the world which follow the British or US
    education system? Some cater specifically for children of ex-
    patriate families, others are open to all-comers. For further
    details on these schools, contact the British Council offices in
    each country — a list of these may be obtained from the British
    Council in London, at 10 Spring Gardens, London SW1A 2BN,
    tel (01) 930 8466.

2. Schools which may combine the curricula of two or more educa-
    tion systems, or provide a bilingual education. At sixth form
    level students may study for the **International Baccalaureate,**
    which gives entry to universities in countries all over the world.
    In EC countries there are the European schools set up to pro-
    vide a multinational education for the children of staff employed
    in the institutions of member countries. Study at these schools
    leads to the **European Baccalaureate.** For addresses see under
    each country heading in Section 2 of this book.

3. So-called **finishing schools.** Many of these today provide an ex-
    tremely relevant curriculum; it may include languages and
    business studies as well as classic subjects such as Cordon Bleu
    cookery. Switzerland is still a highly favoured location. For fur-
    ther information, see the addresses given under the country
    headings in Section 2, or write to the educational trust Gabbitas,
    Truman and Thring, 6-8 Sackville Street, London W1, tel (01)
    734 0161.

Other schemes for young people

EC Young Worker Exchange Programme
This is a scheme open to 18-28 year olds with some vocational training; it takes the form of visits to between three weeks and six months
to another EC country. Shorter projects tend to be merely study
visits, whilst the longer term visits offer the chance for practical work
experience in the country concerned. The idea is to extend knowledge
and skills whilst helping you learn something of the language. For
further details apply to the Central Bureau, Seymour Mews House,
Seymour Mews, London W1H 9PE, or regional offices; see p.171.

World Community Development Service
The WCDS runs an **Educational Visits Scheme** for unskilled young

people who take part in development projects lasting for about six months in India or Sri Lanka. Further details from WCDS, 27 Montagu Road, Botley, Oxford OX2 9AH.

Study visits
The Central Bureau administers **Project Europe** travel bursaries for 16-19 year olds to carry out study visits in EC countries.

LINGUA
This is a very wide-ranging programme designed to improve language teaching and learning in the European Community; it becomes fully operative in the academic year 1991-2. Among its provisions, grants will be available to young people undergoing professional, vocational or technical training for exchanges within the European Community. It is likely that this scheme, when it gets going, will be administered by the Central Bureau for Educational Visits and Exchanges at Seymour Mews House (see above).

Summer camps
These may be organised for young people in various countries and may for example have a musical or sporting theme. Many are listed in Section 2.

Language courses
Of the great variety of language courses available, look out for those designed specifically for the 15-18 age group, as these are likely to provide the most appropriate accommodation and social facilities. Note that some courses only admit over 18 year olds.

OPPORTUNITIES FOR UNDERGRADUATES

First degree courses abroad
Higher education is often organised very differently in different countries. Degree courses are of different lengths, lead to different qualifications, and are taught in different types of institutions. For the purposes of this book, a 'first degree course' means a course leading to an initial higher education qualification. Following EC terminology, and for the sake of brevity, the term 'university' will refer to any educational institution where degree-level studies may be undertaken.

The countries where British students can follow first degree courses are in general limited to those which actively promote cultural and

educational contacts with Britain (eg EC), and those which charge
for higher education on a (semi) commercial basis (eg USA). Other
limiting factors as regards choice of country may be:

- **Knowledge of the language** (see chart p.6). A very good
  knowledge of the language of tuition is needed, not only to
  follow lectures, take notes, and produce written work, but also
  to cope with student life and everyday situations. You may have
  to pass a test in the language before being allowed to enrol for
  a degree course. Some countries offer 'pre-sessional' language
  courses for non-native speakers to bring them up to the required
  level (see **Language Courses, p.27**).

- **Academic qualifications.** Most countries have entrance requirements very similar to those of UK universities, but some
  (notably some US universities) accept less. Others (particularly
  some EC university faculties) may require very good A level
  grades in specific subjects.

- **Finance.** Finding financial support for study outside the UK at
  undergraduate level is very difficult, unless for example you have
  a particular link with a specific country (ie if one of your parents
  is a national, or if you have lived there for a number of years).
  Even if tuition is free, or fees very low, as they are in many countries, you will still need to cover day to day living costs.

- **Immigration.** To gain entry to the country you will need to produce evidence of your means of support for the whole length
  of your course. Some countries require you to agree to return
  home on completing your course. This in turn may limit the value
  to you of the qualifications you obtain. When applying for a
  course, don't forget to leave plenty of time (several months) to
  complete immigration arrangements as the paperwork may be
  quite complicated and some consulates can be very slow in processing applications.

- **The subject you wish to study.** For a variety of reasons countries may not offer the degree you want to take. For example
  Dentistry in Spain is a postgraduate specialisation for graduates
  in Medicine, not a first degree course. The subject you wish to
  study may limit the possibilities open to you in other ways: for
  instance many countries exclude or severely restrict entry of

foreign students to 'professional' degrees, especially law, medicine, and veterinary science, and also in some cases teaching and business studies. Access to purely academic degree courses is generally easier. In some countries the most popular university faculties and departments operate a *numerus clausus* (quotas) policy which limits undergraduate numbers irrespective of whether they are 'foreign' or 'home' students. This can make it even harder for an outsider to get a place.

International Universities

- **American Universities abroad.** Many US universities have campuses or branches abroad, catering both for their own home students wishing to spend a year or semester abroad, whilst gaining credits towards their degree, and for foreign students who wish to obtain an American degree. Many of these are listed in the Countries Section.

- **Schiller International University,** 51 Waterloo Road, London SE1 8TX, tel (01) 928 8484 (Madrid, Paris, Heidelberg and Strasbourg).

- **The International University,** 1301 S. Nolland Road, Independence, Missouri 64055, USA (India and the Far East).

- **US International University,** 10455 Pomerado Road, San Diego, California CA92131, USA; and The Avenue, Bushey, Herts WS2 2LN (Mexico, Africa, Europe).

Doing part of your degree abroad: ERASMUS

More and more universities are offering degrees (not only language degrees, although usually languages do form part of the course) which involve a year or a term spent at another EC university. These courses have been set up under the **European Community Action Scheme for the Mobility of University Students** (ERASMUS), whereby the EC funds finance joint study programmes between EC universities. It is therefore not a scheme directed specifically at individuals, although individuals do obviously benefit from it. ERASMUS has so far enabled more than 500 joint degrees, part-degrees or postgraduate courses to be set up within the European Community, which students apply for through the normal channels in each country.

To find out about Joint Study Programmes in your particular subject, the best sources of information are the normal UCCA and PCAS handbooks, and from there the universities themselves. The Erasmus Bureau in Brussels (rue d'Arlon 15, 1040 Brussels) publishes a complete list of programmes operating each year throughout the Community. When the **LINGUA** programme (see p.19) becomes fully operative, the funds available for promoting language proficiency amongst the university population will be channelled through ERASMUS links and this will give a further boost to the programme: even more students will be able to study abroad for part of their course, or take part in exchanges with universities in other EC countries.

Visiting studentships
This type of arrangement generally lasts one year at undergraduate level. It usually takes the form of a 'year out' from a degree course at a home university; a condition of acceptance as a visiting student is usually that you are already enrolled on a degree course in your own country. Unlike the Joint Study Programmes developed under the ERASMUS scheme above, the year does not form an integral part of your degree. However there's no reason why you shouldn't apply independently to take a 'year out' and spend it as a visiting student abroad (perhaps somewhere further afield than the European Community), irrespective of the type of degree you're doing. The arrangement can take one of two forms, depending on the university:

1. you attend normal undergraduate lectures, as an *auditeur,* ie without sitting the exams.
2. you attend a special course of study designed for foreign students. This may be a 'language and culture' course, or a special 'Junior Year Abroad' program designed for US students (whereby they can gain credits towards their degrees).

In some cases you may find combinations of the above.

Finance
If you're receiving an LEA grant, you may be able to convince your LEA that the time spent abroad as a visiting student is an integral part of your course; for instance language degree courses may have a built in requirement to spend a period of time in the country concerned. In such a case you should be able to continue receiving your grant as normal. Otherwise you will have to seek other sources of funding, as described on p.49 onwards, and, where relevant, under

the Country headings.

How to apply

This will depend very much on whether a pre-arranged scheme exists; if so, you will be able to apply through your home institution, or through central or regional offices whose addresses are given in the Countries section. Otherwise just write directly to the university where you wish to study. Many foreign universities welcome students from Britain on this sort of a basis so don't be put off making enquiries just because there are no pre-existing structures to channel them through.

IAESTE

This is the International Association for the Exchange of Students for Technical Experience. It is a scheme under which higher education students can undertake industrial placements abroad — in one of the 50 countries participating in the scheme. Conditions are that

- you must be already enrolled on a course of higher education in this country;
- the placement must be relevant to that course.

For further details contact the Central Bureau for Educational Visits and Exchanges, Seymour Mews House, Seymour Mews, London W1H 9PE, tel (01) 486 5001, or branches in Edinburgh and Belfast (see p.171).

AIESEC

The International Association of Students of Economics and Business runs an exchange scheme whereby students can undertake traineeships, varying in length from two to eighteen months. There are 59 participating countries. Applicants must be enrolled on, or have recently graduated from, an economics or business studies degree course. Further details from the British office at Seymour Mews House, Seymour Mews, London W1H 9PE.

OPPORTUNITIES FOR POSTGRADUATES

Higher Degrees: possibilities and limitations

Many of the limitations on undergraduate study abroad are lifted in the case of postgraduate study and research, perhaps because there are fewer people chasing this type of opportunity:

- **financial assistance** is more widely available, through bilateral agreements between the UK and a whole range of countries, and through other sources, ranging from local to international organisations (see p.49 and Countries Section for further details).

- a perfect **knowledge of the language** is not of crucial importance at this stage (although it is sometimes a requirement). This is because a working knowledge, or reading knowledge of the language may be good enough for the type of work involved; and because English is widely used in published research.

- **institutions are eager** to attract promising postgraduate students from other countries, and so improve their own standing. Of course, your academic credentials must be excellent.

On the other hand limitations do exist, as follows:

- **financial.** Although sources of funding exist, they may have to be supplemented in some cases. For instance, travel expenses to and from the country may not be included.

- **access** to courses leading to professional qualifications is often still severely restricted.

- because of the structure of university education in some countries, you may need the equivalent of a **Master's degree** in this country before being accepted as a postgraduate abroad.

- **integration** into university life in a foreign country may be more difficult at this stage.

Choice of institution for postgraduates

The choice of institution is crucial for postgraduate work. You will want to find a 'centre of excellence' in your particular field, that offers the right level of support for your studies in terms of teaching and supervisory staff, and of back up facilities (library, laboratories etc). Making a good choice involves undertaking something of a research project in itself. Consult:

- **Directories and guides.** For instance: the *Commonwealth Universities Yearbook,* guides published privately or by the authorities in each country, and international guides, such as information published by the International Bureau of Education, EC, UNESCO, and regional associations. Addresses are given later on in the book.

- **Personal contacts.** Ask teaching and research staff in your own department if they know of any 'centres of excellence' in your subject in other countries, or in the country where you wish to study.

- Refer to **published research and articles.** If the famous Professor X from the University of Y published a key piece of research in your field, it's a small step to check if s/he's still there.

For postgraduate study, **application** is usually directed to the university concerned. There may or may not be an official application form, and you will have to supply all or some of the following documents:

1. Degree certificate.
2. Academic transcripts (details of the courses which made up your degree on a year by year basis, and results obtained).
3. CV.
4. Details of any publications.
5. The research proposal, if relevant, or details of your areas of interest.
6. Letter(s) of support from your previous/current institution.

European Universities
The **College of Europe** in Bruges and the **European University Institute** in Florence both offer postgraduates research opportunities on European themes. For further details, see under Belgium and Italy in Section 2.

Overseas Development Administration Postgraduate Training Awards Scheme
The ODA runs a postgraduate training scheme for people seriously interested in development issues and intending to work overseas under the **British Aid Programme.** Applicants must be graduates but the specific degree subjects vary according to circumstances. Further details from Appointments Officer, Room AH358, Postgraduate Training Awards Scheme, Overseas Development Administration,

Abercrombie House, Eaglesham Road, East Kilbride, Glasgow G75 8AE.

Short specialist courses

Short specialist courses for postgraduates from all countries are held at universities throughout the world. Again, English is often used as a medium. The best source of information on these, apart from your own university department (and of course, Section 2 below!), is *Study Abroad* (see p.174).

Short courses for language teachers are organised under the auspices of HM Inspectorate in France, Germany, Italy and Spain — also in Italy and Greece for Classics teachers.

ERASMUS

Many of the Joint Study Programmes developed under the ERASMUS scheme (see above) are for postgraduate study.

Commonwealth Schemes

See chapter on Commonwealth in Section 2.

OPPORTUNITIES FOR POST-EXPERIENCE AND MATURE STUDENTS

International Summer Schools

These are usually held in university premises during the long vacation and may be specialist or generalist in nature. Many use English as a medium. See Countries Section for further details.

Study visits

These are generally organised on an ad hoc basis for individuals or groups who wish to study aspects of a particular country and do not follow set courses of study open to the general public. However they are worth mentioning here as funds are available for study visits to certain countries (see Countries Section). The addresses given in the Countries Section will also be useful for the purposes of organising study visits.

The Central Bureau for Education Visits and Exchanges (see p.171) provides funds for specially approved study visits abroad, mainly in the area of educational co-operation.

EC Young Worker Exchange Programme

For 18-28 year olds. See p.18.

Language courses

See below.

LANGUAGE COURSES

Language courses of some sort or another exist in almost every country. They are organised with a variety of aims in mind, ranging from an earnest desire to promote national or regional cultures to making a quick buck out of unsuspecting foreigners. Basically the following sorts of course exist, and your choice will depend on your own reasons for wanting to learn the language (bearing in mind that not all countries offer every type of course):

- **Pre-sessional courses.** Usually run by universities during the long vacations and open only to students who have been offered a place for the forthcoming academic year and need to improve their language skills before taking it up.

- **University summer courses.** Again run by, or in collaboration with, universities during the summer months, but open to a wider public. Sometimes these are combined with international summer schools (see below) which cater for other interests besides just 'language and culture'.

- **Courses in universities throughout the year.** These are usually variations on 'language and culture' themes for students who already have a working or intermediate knowledge of the language. However, some universities offer 'pre-degree language years' to foreign students and here the emphasis is more on using the language for academic purposes. Sometimes you may be able to attend for just a term or a semester rather than for the whole academic year.

- **Private courses run by language schools.** The range of these can be immense both in terms of type and quality of course. When choosing see checklist on p.29.

How to apply for a language course

Independent applications
The most basic information you need to start with is a contact address and or telephone number — many of these appear in the Countries Section. More detailed lists appear in:

- *Study Holidays,* published by the Central Bureau for Educational Visits and Exchanges (see p.171 for address), price £5.50.

Gives details of language courses in Europe only.

● *CILT Language and Culture Guides.* A series published by the Centre for Information on Language Teaching and Research, Regent's College, Inner Circle, Regent's Park, London NW1 4NS, tel (01) 486 8221, covering all the major world languages.

You will need in any case to write or telephone for an application form; the school will send you at the same time all the latest information on courses, prices and dates. You can then send off your application, together with a booking fee/deposit if required. Having booked a course, you will then have to make your own travel, visa and insurance arrangements.

Applying through an agency
If you are unsure about dealing directly with an overseas institution, or if you would like a language 'package' with travel included, or if you would simply like someone else to do the work for you, you can book a language course through an agency in the UK. Agencies which deal with one country only are given in the appropriate country section later on in the book; the following commercial organizations handle bookings for courses in a whole range of countries:

Cultural and Educational Services Abroad, 44 Sydney Street, Brighton, East Sussex BN1 4EP. Tel (0273) 683304. France, Belgium, Austria, Germany, Italy, Spain.

Educational Travel Ltd, 236 South Norwood Hill, London SE25 6AZ. Tel (01) 653 3388. Courses in France, Germany and Spain for GCSE and A level students.

Educational Travel Service, 82 Newlands Road, London SW16 4SH. Tel (01) 653 8467. Groups only, throughout Europe.

Euro-Academy Ltd, 77a George St, Croydon, Surrey CR0 1LD. Tel (01) 681 2905. Ages 12-26 in France, Germany, Italy and Spain.

Eurolanguage Ltd, Greyhound House, 23-24 George Street, Richmond, Surrey TW9 1HY. Tel (01) 940 1087. France.

Euroyouth, 301 Westborough Road, Westcliff, Southend-on-Sea, Essex SS0 9PT. Tel (0702) 341434. Germany, Italy, Austria, Spain, France, and Belgium.

International Study Programmes, The Manor, Hazleton, Cheltenham GL54 4EB. Tel (0451) 60379. Mainly courses for 'young' people in Germany and Spain.

John Galleymore, 24 High Street, Portsmouth, Hampshire PO1 2LS.
Tel (0705) 824095. Austria, France, Italy, Spain, Tunisia and USSR.

Language Studies London, 10-12 James Street, London W1M 5HN.
Germany, Spain.

NST Ltd, 13-17 All Hallows Road, Bispham, Blackpool, Lancs. Tel
(0253) 52525. France and Germany. Mainly school groups.

Progressive Tours, 12 Porchester Place, London W2 2BS. Tel (01)
262 1676. USSR and other socialist countries.

The Robertson Organisation, 44 Willoughby Road, London NW3.
Tel (01) 435 4907. France, Germany and Spain. Ages up to 19 only.

Courses can also be booked through language teaching organisations
in this country which have branches abroad:

Eurocentres, 21 Meadowcourt Road, London SE3 9EU. Tel (01) 318
5633. France, Belgium, Germany, Spain.

Inlingua, 8-10 Rotton Park Road, Edgbaston, Birmingham B16 9JJ.
Tel (021) 454 0204, and 55-61 Portland Road, Brighton, East Sussex
BN3 5DQ. Tel (0273) 721612. France, Belgium, Italy, Portugal,
Spain.

International House, 106 Piccadilly, London W1V 9FL. Tel (01) 491
2598. Germany, Hungary, Italy, Portugal, Spain.

See also *Home from Home,* a Central Bureau publication (price
£3.50) listing organisations which offer homestays with foreign
families, some of which also offer language courses.

**Checklist of points to bear in mind when choosing a language
course**

- Is the course appropriate to your level of ability/prior knowledge
  of the language?
- What aspects does it emphasise, eg conversation, languages or
  business purposes, language for academic purposes, culture and
  literature, culture and society?
- Does it offer you the chance to obtain any nationally or inter-
  nationally recognised diplomas?

- What type of teaching methodology is used? Traditional chalk and talk and textual commentary, audio-visual and lab work, or 'communicative' methods?
- Will it emphasise grammar or communicative aspects of the language?
- How big are the classes?
- How are the groups organised? Will you be in the same group right through your course, or will there constantly be students leaving and joining the group? (there can be pros and cons to both).
- How competent are the teachers? What qualifications do they have?
- How many hours per week/day does the course involve?
- What other activities are organised, eg excursions, visits, social occasions?
- Location. Is it in a town/city/country area/resort that will offer you plenty of interest?
- Will the course give you a chance to meet local people?
- What is the physical character of the institution: modern/old, spacious/small, luxurious/plain?
- Accommodation: what sort of accommodation is provided? Is it included in the cost? Would family, residential or hotel accommodation suit you best?
- Meals? Are they included in the cost?
- Finally cost — taking all the above factors into account, does the course represent good value for money?

Applying to study abroad

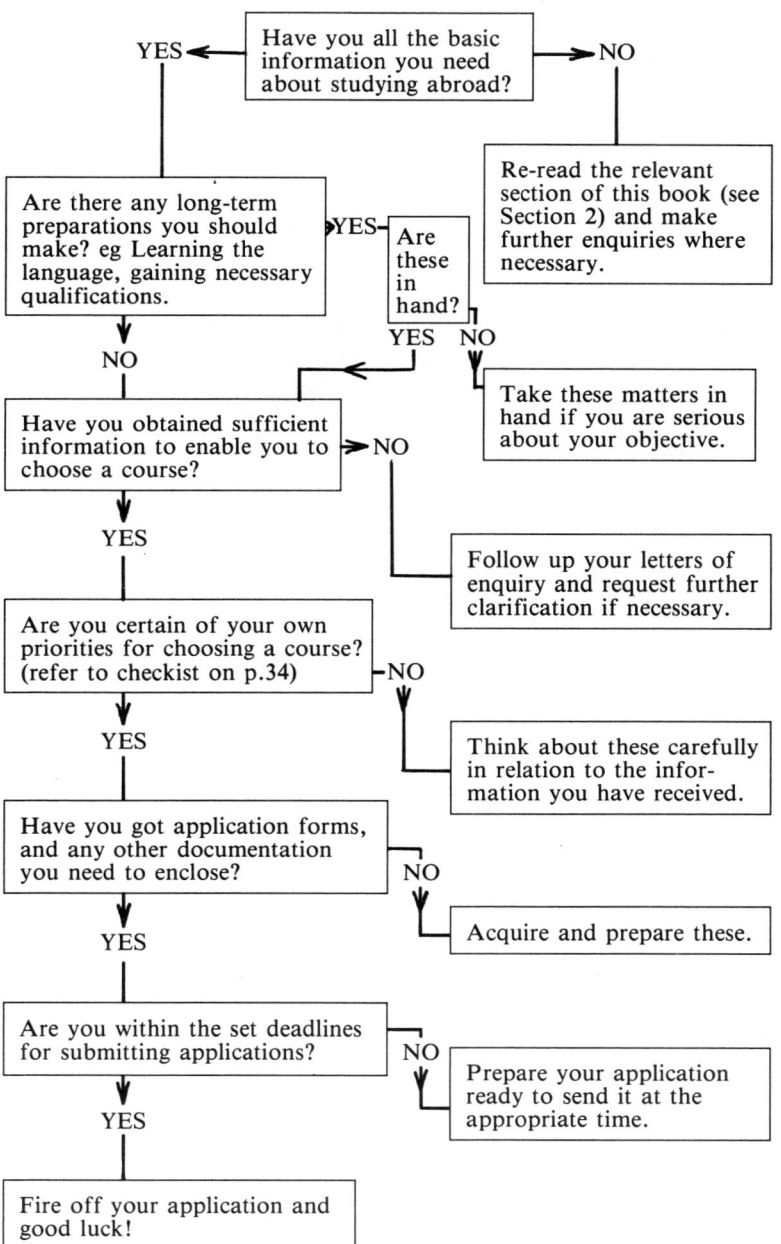

3
Getting a Place
on a Course Abroad

Now you're sure you want to study abroad, and you've got an idea about what sort of course might be for you, and where, it's time to start making those ideas a reality. This chapter will show, stage by stage, how to go about getting your name on a letter of acceptance.

LONG-TERM PREPARATIONS

If your aim is to take your degree abroad, you may have to think about preparing for it several years in advance, perhaps at the stage when you decide what A levels to study. A good preparation can be the International Baccalaureate course, which takes the place of A levels, so perhaps you might look into doing that. The IB office will supply a list of schools which offer this. Learning the language can be an essential pre-requisite to studying abroad, and this again is a long-term project. Your school, college or local adult education institute is the best place to start learning the language.

Stage 1: getting information

Depending on what course you want to study, the information contained in Section 2 of this book may be enough for you to start firing off letters of enquiry requesting further details of courses and application forms. If your requirements are very specific though, or if you're going to a country such as the United States, where myriad opportunities exist, you'll have to do a bit of preliminary research yourself; use the directories of courses, central information offices and useful addresses referred to under each country heading. In some cases, the Embassy of the country concerned may have all the initial information you will need, in others you will have to write direct to the country concerned. Make sure you leave plenty of time for this. It's never too soon to start collecting this initial information and comparing the options available.

Stage 2: preselection of courses

The next step is to shortlist the courses you could be interested in. How many you shortlist will depend on how sure you are about the type of course you want to do: if you're still not sure whether you want to do architecture or business studies, whether to do it in Italy or the United States, and whether or not you need to do a language course first, you may end up writing to a dozen or so institutions. However if you've already narrowed the field, two or three should be enough.

Stage 3: the letter of enquiry

These are usually sent direct to the institution concerned, but in some cases there may be a central information office which can send you further information and application forms. In these cases, though, you may still want to contact the university as well, to be sure of getting all the details about what you'll actually be studying. Make your initial enquiries *well in advance* of when you intend to start the course, ie up to 18 months beforehand.

Include as much relevant information as possible about yourself (see checklist below). This will not only help the authorities to assess your situation, but is sometimes of very specific importance, for instance in deciding which type of application form to send you.

Checklist of essential details to include in initial enquiry:

- Your name, address and telephone number.
- Present qualifications and projected results of exams you still have to take.
- Your nationality and normal country of residence.
- What course(s) you are interested in and why (briefly!).
- How you intend supporting yourself financially. (Whilst it is permissible to ask about financial aid available, your application won't be taken seriously if it is couched in terms of 'send me all the information on how I can study free in your country'.)
- International reply coupon — available from Post Offices. Not essential, but a point of courtesy which encourages a helpful response.

Stage 4: studying the literature

It can't be stressed too strongly that, when you receive replies to your letters, you should read the literature thoroughly. First go through the details of the course with a finetooth comb; try to pick out not only the things they tell you, but the things they *don't* tell you. Think about the course content, how it will be taught, the number of hours study it will require; how will it be assessed? What qualification will it give you? Then look at the entrance requirements, especially for foreign students, and the cost of the course. Are there any special immigration requirements for the country concerned? Are any grants available? If anything is not clear, ask for clarification now. Embassies may be able to help here, but if not don't be afraid to make a quick phone call direct to the place which sent you the information. If you don't speak the language, get someone who can to do it for you. It really is worth taking trouble over this stage to be sure that your experience of studying abroad will be successful. Eliminate any courses which don't come up to scratch or are unsuitable for other reasons, and if necessary go back to stage 2 and make a different selection of courses.

Course checklist:

- Syllabus: what exactly will be studied, and at what level?
- Teaching: how will the course be taught?
- Duration and number of hours study required?
- Assessment: continuous, or by examination?
- Qualification: what sort of qualification will the course give you?
- Entrance requirements, especially for foreign students. By examination?
- Language requirements?
- Cost of course?
- Availability of grants?
- Immigration requirements?
- Characteristics of university/teaching institution?
- Location — ease of travel?
- Accommodation and facilities?

Stage 5: making your application
You should now be left with a handful of courses you seriously want to apply for. How many you actually apply for will depend on how likely you are to be accepted. If you are applying for a commercial language course, and have to send a booking fee, you will obviously only apply to the one, assuming you are within the time limit given for applications. However for some university courses you may want to apply for four or five, to be on the safe side. *Read the instructions*

carefully, including the small print. What details do you have to put where? Where do you have to send it? When is the closing date? Do you have to send various copies to different places? What enclosures are required? To avoid making a mess of the form make a photocopy of it first and fill that in; when you are satisfied copy the details on to the original. Before sending off your application, make a copy of it. Do you need to apply for a visa? You may need one (initially at least) to show the immigration authorities. Send your application by registered post if you think this is necessary.

Stage 6: following up the application
By the time you send off your application you should have clear in your mind the timetable of events to follow:

- When you are likely to receive a reply (so you know when to chase them up if you don't).

- When you should apply for any grants.

- When your UK qualifications will be verified. Do you have to take any special steps to get them officially recognised by the foreign authorities? When will you need to inform them of the results of A levels or other exams?

- When you have to take any entrance exams. Can you take these in the UK or do you have to travel to the country concerned to sit them? When? Make sure they don't clash with your A level exams.

- If selection is by interview, when you are likely to be called for this.

- How you will be informed of arrangements for enrolment.

- When you will have to pay any fees.

Keep a note of this timetable, and chase up any item which does not fall into place at the right time.

Stage 7: acceptance or rejection
If you've read the literature carefully, you should by now have some idea of how likely you are to be accepted. If the institution concerned welcomes foreign students (especially if it is a commercial organisation), if you fulfil the entry requirements and have made your application exactly according to the instructions, you will obviously

have a very good chance of being accepted. When that acceptance letter comes, keep it in a safe place (you will need it for immigration purposes when travelling to the country), and *don't forget to accept the offer — in writing*. Now's the time to chase up those grant applications. A place at a university can be of little value if you can't afford to take it up!

You may have applied to an institution where there is intense competition for places from within the country concerned as well as from foreign students like yourself; if so don't take it too hard if instead of an offer of a place you receive a polite letter of rejection. It was worth the try, and other opportunities for study abroad will come up, perhaps at a later stage in your career.

USING AN AGENCY: THE PROS AND CONS

For some types of courses, especially language courses and school year abroad programmes, there are agencies which can handle your application and get you a place. It can be a very good idea to use one of these; it can save you an awful lot of work, as long as your own particular needs can be met by the agency concerned. Here's a brief guide to the pros and cons of using an agency:

Advantages
- Saves time.
- Saves trouble and possible frustration in trying to contact foreign institutions.
- May not necessarily be more expensive.
- Agency is aware of all options/pitfalls of a particular type of course and should be able to provide useful advice and guidance.
- Travel and insurance may be included as a package.
- If something goes wrong, the agency may take responsibility and sort things out for you.

Disadvantages
- Reduces range of courses available.
- Usually only arranges private-sector courses.
- Arrangements cannot usually be tailor-made to *your* requirements (for instance you may have to compromise over dates, or travel with a group).
- Agency may act as a barrier and prevent free flow of information between you and the institution concerned, giving rise to misapprehensions.

● Can be more expensive than making arrangements privately.

Conclusions

If you're going to use an agency make sure that it:

1. offers sufficient choice in terms of the type of course you want, at the right time of year, in the right location etc.
2. does not charge inflated prices (its profits should come from commission from institutions, not from you the consumer).

4
Preparing for
Study Overseas

Having accepted your place, what next? It's now time to start looking at all the practical arrangements you will need to make.

VISAS/IMMIGRATION

When reading the course information sent to you, you will probably have come across a section on visa or immigration requirements. This is something that needs sorting out well in advance, as Consulates can be very slow in processing applications for visas or special residence permits. In general terms, the further afield you are going, the more complicated will be the immigration procedures. If you are just going on a short language course (less than three months) to an EC country you won't have to prepare any special documents; just make sure your passport is up to date. However even countries with close ties with the UK can require visas or special residence permits for students staying for longer periods. Obtain all the necessary information from the Consular Section of the Embassy concerned (addresses are given under each country heading in Section 2 of this book) and apply in good time for all the necessary documents to be prepared. You may even have to do it before receiving the final letter of acceptance.

Documents likely to be required

- Passport valid for at least six months from date of travel.
- Letter of acceptance from the institution where you intend to study (if this hasn't arrived yet a copy of your application may suffice meanwhile, however you will normally have to supply firm evidene of acceptance before the visa will be issued).
- Passport sized photographs.
- Multiple application forms.

- Evidence of how you will support yourself whilst in the country. This may be for example an official letter confirming a grant from whatever source, or evidence of funds available in the country concerned (you may have to open a bank account and transfer money there in advance).
- Letter of support from your home institution, or from someone in the country concerned.
- Academic certificates.
- Declaration that you will return home once you have completed your course.
- Practically anything else that the relevant authorities can dream up.

TRAVEL ARRANGEMENTS

How are you going to travel? Now's the time to start thinking about booking your tickets. Many foreign governments have official tourist offices in this country. They cannot actually book your tickets for you, but they can supply lots of useful information free of charge, including lists of travel agents specialising in cheap or educational travel to the country. Addresses of these are given under each country heading in Section 2. Also, remember that as a student you may be eligible for special travel concessions. Specialist student travel agencies in this country include:

STA Travel, 74 Old Brompton Road, London SW7 3LQ. Tel (01) 581 1022.

World Student Travel, 37-38 Store Street, London WC1. Tel (01) 580 7733.

For onward travel once you are in the country concerned, there may be specialist agencies belonging to the **Federation of International Youth Travel Organisations** (FIYTO) or **International Student Travel Conference** — these are listed under each country heading in Section 2.

If you are flying, try to book your flight at least two months before departure, and make sure you have your tickets by a fortnight before.

Travel: sources of information

- National Tourist Offices (see addresses in Countries Section).
- Student travel agencies.
- Specialist travel agencies (agencies which offer language course packages are listed on p.28).

ACCOMMODATION

Student accommodation is a problem all over the world. Perhaps surprisingly, it is especially so in countries with large thriving higher education sectors, where accommodation costs may seriously affect your budget. For instance in Germany (Federal Republic) although tuition is free, student accommodation is very scarce and costs may be astronomical. In the literature sent you by the institution concerned, there will no doubt be a section on accommodation arrangements. Go back and read this again now. What sort of accommodation is available? Is it included with the course? — usually in the case of short courses this is so. If not are there any facilities at the institution concerned for finding accommodation for foreign students? Can this be done in advance, or will it be up to you to find somewhere to live when you arrive? If there is anything you can do in advance, do so now. If nothing is arranged for you, you might consider phoning any contact you may have in the country to see if they can help. If nothing can be done, ask the tourist office for a list of cheap hotels or bed and breakfast accommodation, so that at least you have somewhere to make for when you first arrive.

Types of student accommodation

- Halls of residence
- Self-catering university accommodation
- Privately rented accommodation
- Sharing — see student notice boards
- With families.

INSURANCE

Many countries have **reciprocal social security** agreements with the UK. This means that you should get some free or reduced cost medical attention, albeit limited to emergencies in many cases. Details are given in leaflet SA40 *Before you go: A Traveller's Guide to Health,* available from the DSS, tel (01) 407 5522 etc 6711. Some countries have special student medical insurance schemes, which you are required or encouraged to join before embarking on a course of study. Do examine the insurance situation fully before you go; if you think you may need extra cover, contact: **International Student Insurance Service,** Endsleigh Insurance Services Ltd, Endsleigh House, Ambrose Street, Cheltenham Spa, Gloucestershire GL50 3NR, tel (0242) 36151, or local Endsleigh branches. The importance of having good insurance cover cannot be stressed too strongly. Before you go, find out the name of the Foreign Student Adviser or other person to contact for any problems which arise once you are there.

VACCINATIONS

Depending on what country you are going to, vaccinations against certain diseases may be compulsory or recommended. DSS leaflet SA40 (see above) gives full details of these, together with advice on protecting your health whilst abroad. Leave yourself plenty of time to arrange these.

MONEY

If you will be getting a grant, now's also the time to get confirmation of this. *When* exactly will the money be available and *how* exactly will it be paid to you? Will you need extra funds to cover the first few weeks? Work out a budget of how much money you think you will need for your stay. Include:

● Tuition fees
● Registration fee
● Examination fees
● Student union affiliation fee
● Health insurance contribution
● Extra insurance
● Travel costs
● Immigration charges
● Accommodation (plus deposit in some cases)
● Food
● Books and equipment
● Day to day expenses: bus fares, socialising, toiletries etc

Have you sufficient funds to cover all these expenses? If not go to the checklist on p.49 and see if there are any other ways you could boost your finances.

You also need to think about how you are going to take the money abroad with you. Will you take it with you (in cash or travellers cheques), send it by bank transfer, or use Eurocheques or credit cards to access your account from abroad? Will you use only cash, or will you open a bank account in the country concerned? Whatever you decide, you will need to order some local currency now to take with you. Also, it is well worth having access to a credit card (Visa, Access, etc) abroad, if at all possible. It can see you out of some awkward situations, especially in the early days before you get your cash flow sorted out. Keep credit cards safely though, and make a note of their details and the emergency numbers to phone in case they are lost or stolen.

PAPERWORK

You can now start to gather together all the vital documents you will need for travel and study abroad:

- Passport valid for at least six months
- Visa or special residence permit
- Letter of acceptance on the course
- Any other information sent you from the university or other institution, especially campus diagrams, lists of useful addresses, timetables for registration etc. These will be vitally important in the first few days
- Grant — letter of confirmation or cheque
- Other money in whatever form, including some currency
- Tickets and other travel documents
- Insurance
- Student Identity card. These are available from student travel offices (see p.39) and offer useful concessions on travel, accommodation, entry to museums, etc.
- Address and telephone number of nearest British Consulate or Embassy.

You may also want to take:

- Address book
- Maps and street plans (if you have difficulty obtaining these, contact the national tourist office)
- Phrase book (if necessary)
- This guide (or photocopy of relevant pages)
- Background information about the country/region concerned. (Ask the tourist office for free literature).
- Radio.
- Simple first aid pack including painkillers, elastoplast (you may get blisters tramping the streets in the first few days!), antiseptic, and other basics.

Sorting out your accommodation

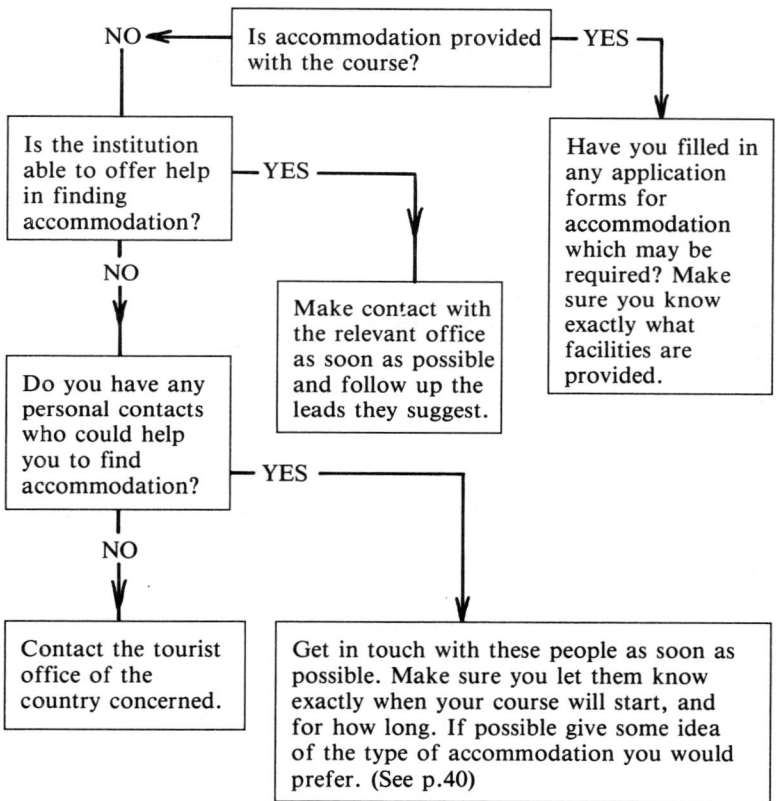

NO ← Is accommodation provided with the course? — YES

Is the institution able to offer help in finding accommodation? — YES

Have you filled in any application forms for accommodation which may be required? Make sure you know exactly what facilities are provided.

Make contact with the relevant office as soon as possible and follow up the leads they suggest.

NO

Do you have any personal contacts who could help you to find accommodation? — YES

NO

Contact the tourist office of the country concerned.

Get in touch with these people as soon as possible. Make sure you let them know exactly when your course will start, and for how long. If possible give some idea of the type of accommodation you would prefer. (See p.40)

5
What to Do on Arrival

Having arrived at your destination, your first two major tasks are:

● checking into your accommodation
● registering for your course

Give these top priority. If you've organised yourself so well that you've arrived a few days early, you may find you cannot register immediately. This can be frustrating; you are naturally eager to sign up and start classes right away. However, the intervening time can be usefully spent checking things out (read all noticeboards in sight!), so by the time your course commences your accommodation is sorted out and you know:

● how to get from it to the teaching institution
● how to get to the town centre and shops
● exactly where and when you have to register
● (if possible) your timetable, and where classes are to be held (or at least where you must report)
● where to exchange or withdraw money
● where to eat

If your course lasts more than a couple of months or so, you may also have to register with the civil authorities, letting them know your address. You may also like to:

1. sign up with the British Consulate (if there's one reasonably near);

2. sign on with any student organisations — these can provide useful contacts in the first few days;

3. visit the local student travel organisation, if there is one (addresses are given under each country heading in Section 2). These can provide a useful point of contact with other students, and for information on accommodation, social activities, clubs, excursions, meetings, student concessions etc;

4. sign on with a doctor, or at least find out where you can get medical help when needed.

All in all, there's plenty to occupy those first few difficult days when you're trying to get your bearings and settle in.

TROUBLESHOOTING

However well organised you are, problems may crop up, perhaps through no fault of your own. Here's some advice for dealing with them.

If you run out of money

First, analyse the problem. Have you really miscalculated your budget, or have you just got a temporary cash-flow crisis?

Cash-flow problems

If it's just a case of your grant being slow to come through or a bank taking over-long to process a cheque, then at least you know that, although things may be tight for a few days, time will resolve the problem. Meanwhile, spend as little money as possible; get credit where you can, and try to speed up that cash in whatever way possible. See your foreign student adviser or tutor in charge; universities may have a hardship fund from which they can make short term loans in cases such as these.

Budgetary problems

However, if your problem is shaping up to be more serious, and you find you just haven't enough money to get by, week by week, you will have to take some definite action. Don't waste time blaming yourself or anyone else; the point is to find a practical solution. You will either have to increase your income, decrease your outgoings, or both.

First look at your **expenditure.** Has it been abnormally high in the first few weeks, with extra and once-off expenses that won't reoccur throughout the rest of the course? Can you offset any initial high expenditure by cutting your budget for future weeks? Is one

single item on your budget proving more costly than you had ima-
gined? Can you make savings on this in any way, for instance by
sharing costs with other students?

Now look at your **income.** It is unlikely that any grants will be
open to you at this stage, but there may be hardship funds to help
foreign students hit by fluctuations in exchange rates for example.
It is worthwhile enquiring about these. You should also go into the
question of work. You may, on a student visa, be prevented from
working full time, but you may be able to work part-time for a few
hours each week and earn that extra bit of cash. Even if this too
is banned, you may be able to boost funds by doing 'unofficial' work
such as baby-sitting, giving English conversation classes, or private
coaching. Ask around about these possibilities. If you're near the
end of your course, and you've just simply run out of money, then
perhaps the best thing is just to get cash sent from home. You can
get a cash advance on a credit card, or you can arrange for a bank
overdraft, or you can borrow from friends or family. If you need
money transferred from home, you will need to give the name and
address of a bank where you wish to receive it. Try not to transfer
money more than once, to avoid excessive commission charges.

If you run into trouble with the authorities
If you are unlucky enough to be arrested or run into trouble with
the authorities in any other way, whether through your own fault
or not, you should inform the nearest British Consulate or Embassy,
and they will advise you on what you should do. Make sure you
always have their number easily to hand.

If you are robbed or attacked
Report the incident to the police, preferably in the company of someone who speaks the language well.

If you have problems with your course
Don't be too quick to decide you are 'having trouble' with your
course. Remember, you are in a different education system, perhaps
working in a different language from the one you are used to; it's
bound to take time to adjust. If you continue to doubt your ability
to cope with the course, or its suitability, then ask your adviser, tutor,
or course director for help. You may be able to overcome any problems with extra coaching, remedial language classes, or perhaps by
transfer to another course or group.

If you have accommodation problems

Student accommodation problems can be the end. Your rooms may be too noisy, too far away, too dirty, too uncomfortable, or you may not get on well with your fellow-tenants. You may be desperate to change, but find alternative accommodation hard to find, or too expensive. If your problems are not overwhelming, you may decide to put up with them for the duration of your course. Or perhaps you can dream up some practical ways of easing the situation, like buying ear plugs or organising a cleaning rota. However if you're actually prevented from sleeping, studying or generally keeping yourself fit and healthy, then you should certainly consider a move. First try any student accommodation or welfare offices that exist. They may at least be able to supply a list of addresses for you to follow up. Scan college noticeboards. Put up your own ad if necessary. Read the advertisements in local papers, shop windows, etc. Ask around. Let people know that you are looking for alternative accommodation, without making them feel put upon. Work at it, and before long something should turn up.

If you fall ill

Assess the gravity of the situation, with a doctor's help if necessary. A bout of flu when you are alone in a foreign country will be unpleasant, but does not call for British Embassy intervention! If you have to take to your bed for a few days, make sure

- you have plenty of drinking water;
- someone, somewhere, knows where you are (preferably a tutor or fellow student).

If you do need urgent medical treatment, make sure you have a copy of your insurance policy. If you have to pay for the treatment and then claim it off your insurance policy, do so however you can, and make sure you are given receipts. In an extreme situation the British Consulate or Embassy will come to your aid and arrange for you to be returned to the UK if necessary.

If you experience 'culture shock'

Don't be embarrassed by feelings of culture shock. However tolerant we are of other cultures, there are always certain aspects of our own which we hold dear and never wish to let go of; this is perfectly natural, so accept culture shock and let time be the best cure of it. Adapt as best you can, and look around for like-minded people with whom to share and discuss your experiences. No culture is monolithic; wherever you are you are likely to find people around of a wide range of opinions, some of whom will be easier for you to get on with than others. Join clubs or societies where you are likely to meet such people. Expatriate clubs can provide temporary relief, but don't depend on them to the exclusion of all that is of value and interest in the host country.

If you are lonely or homesick

A little homesickness is quite normal. In fact one of the most positive experiences of studying abroad is that it allows you to reflect on your home life and put it into perspective. But try not to become too introspective, and make the most of the present experience whilst you have the chance. Plan each week ahead, so you can see how you're going to spend each day. If there are any gaps, try to organise activities to fill them usefully. How about using a weekend to go on a sightseeing trip with a fellow student? If it is the evenings which are a problem, how about offering to prepare a meal or meet someone for drinks? Try to make the effort to get involved with the people you are with. Don't stay locked in your room feeling sorry for yourself!

Financial preparations for overseas study

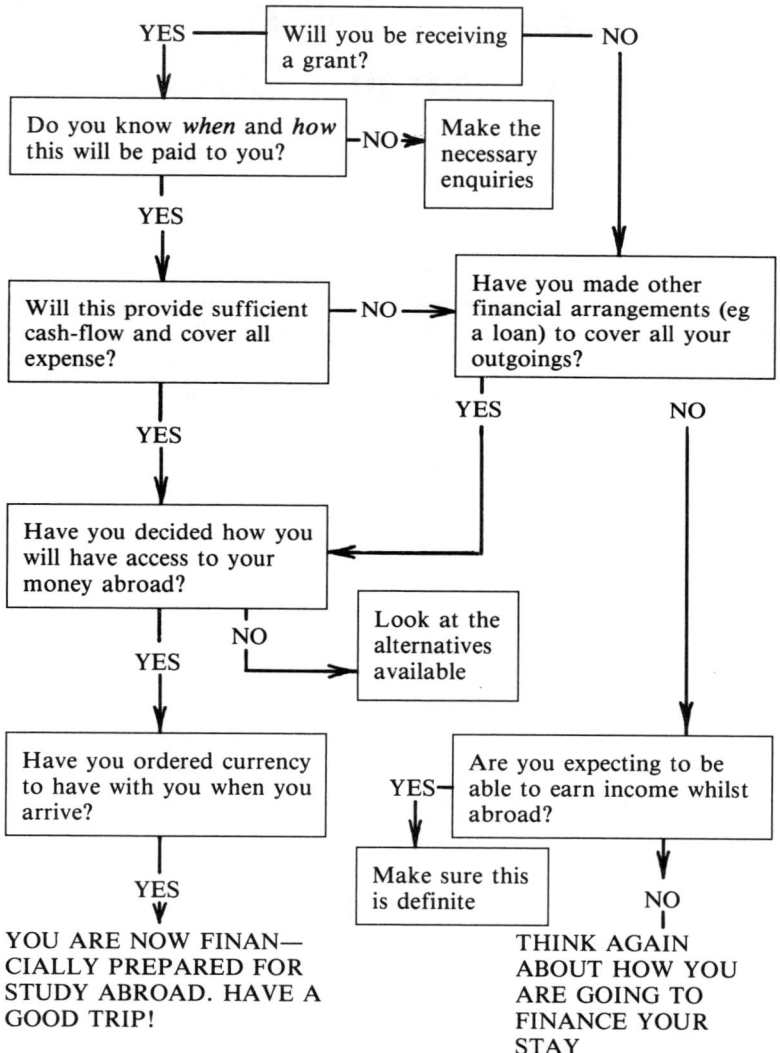

English-Speaking and Commonwealth Countries

If you regard yourself as an inveterate monolingual, you will probably have turned to this chapter automatically. Indeed, there are many points in favour of studying abroad in an English-speaking country (apart from the obvious one of being able to understand what people are saying!).

- You feel more at home and it's easier to find your way around;
- Access to books and information is easier;
- There are generally established links between countries which share our common language;
- These countries tend to have friendly relations with Britain, making immigration procedures more straightforward.

However, don't rule out the possibility of studying abroad in non-English speaking countries simply on linguistic grounds. Other countries (for instance Israel) use English fairly widely in higher education, and at postgraduate level, particularly in scientific fields, this tendency is even more widespread. Why be put off by the idea of learning a foreign language anyway? The experience of studying abroad can be doubly enriching if it means you also learn to speak another language. Anyone can learn a foreign language, there's no magic to it, just a bit of effort needed. Knowing another language is a valuable asset that's becoming more and more of a necessity as we develop closer ties with other countries and carry out more and more of our business on the international stage. If you are thinking of learning a language, the best place to do this is in the country concerned, and details of many such courses are given in subsequent chapters of this book. So even if English is your sole language — at present — don't restrict yourself to reading just this chapter: have a look at the sections on non-English speaking countries too.

The countries covered in this chapter divide into 'developed' English-speaking countries such as Australia, Canada and Ireland, and the 'non-developed' Commonwealth countries, where English is widely used as an official language. Of the countries included in this chapter, Australia, Canada and the USA offer the most wide-ranging opportunities for study abroad, although other countries can be promising for pursuing particular fields of study, tropical medicine, foreign languages, development studies and so forth.

Information on University Courses

An indispensable source is the *Commonwealth Universities Yearbook,* a substantial tome packed with all the basic facts on Commonwealth universities — what courses they run, what staff they have, what their admission requirements are. Consult this book as a first step in your public or university library.

Grants

The Commonwealth Scholarship and Fellowship Plan. The more financially able Commonwealth governments offer awards to UK graduates for postgraduate studies in their countries lasting from one to three years. Candidates must be nominated through the Association of Commonwealth Universities. Contact the Joint Secretaries, Commonwealth Scholarship Commission, ACU, 36 Gordon Square, London WC1 0PE.

For details of other sources of funding, see the following ACU publications, which are updated every year or so:

Scholarships Guide for Commonwealth Postgraduate Students
Research Opportunities in Commonwealth Developing Countries
Financial Aid for First Degree Study at Commonwealth Universities

Only the countries which offer specific study possibilities are dealt with individually here. For the rest, you should either make contact directly with the institution you are interested in (after consulting the *Commonwealth Universities Yearbook*), or seek further information from the relevant High Commission in London. Addresses are given at the end of this chapter.

Commonwealth youth exchanges

The **Commonwealth Youth Exchange Council**, 18 Fleet Street, London EC4Y 1AA, tel (01) 353 3901, promotes reciprocal visits and exchanges for groups between Britain and other Commonwealth countries.

Professional visits and exchanges within the Commonwealth

There are a number of Commonwealth professional organisations (for architects, journalists, nurses, librarians and others) which promote professional collaboration, exchanges and visits between Commonwealth countries. Further details may be obtained from the **Commonwealth Foundation,** Secretariat, Marlborough House, Pall Mall, London SW1Y 5HX, tel (01) 839 3411. The Foundation also offers Fellowships for short term study or visits by professional people throughout the Commonwealth.

Commonwealth Youth Programme

Under this scheme 35 to 40 bursaries are offered annually to youth workers to attend Regional Youth Training Centres in India, Guyana, Zambia and Fiji. Further details from Commonwealth Youth Programme, Marlborough House, Pall Mall, London SW1Y 5HX. Tel (01) 839 3411.

AUSTRALIA

See also introductory section on studying in the Commonwealth p.50.

There are 21 universities in Australia which accept foreign students at graduate level only.

Language of tuition English.
Academic year February/March to October/November.
Best contacts for information
● Association of Commonwealth Universities (ACU), John Foster House, 36 Gordon Square, London WC1H 0PE. Tel (01 387 8572.
● Australian High Commission: Australia House, Strand, London WC2B 4LA Tel (01) 438 8000.

Postgraduate

All Australian universities offer both Masters and Doctoral degrees, although not necessarily in all faculties. For general information see the ACU leaflet *Graduate Study at Australian Universities.* For detailed information about specific institutions see the *Commonwealth Universities Yearbook,* available in university libraries, and in the ACU Library at the above address (make an appointment first).

Contact
The universities themselves. Applications must be made through the Overseas Student Office of the Australian Department of Education, PO Box 25, Woden, ACT, Australia 2606.

Entrance requirements Good Bachelor's degree, or Master's degree for PhD.

Cost
Costs depend on whether the place is subsidised or non-subsidised. All university departments have quotas on the number of subsidised places they can offer to foreign students. The subsidy is up to 50% of the full cost — students must find the rest from other sources — and there is in addition an annual Overseas Student Charge and an Administration Charge. The ACU estimates costs would be in the range $A12,000 to $A16,000 per year, excluding travel. There are no quotas for non-subsidised (full fee) places, but costs are of course higher.

Grants
About 60 awards are given annually under the Commonwealth Scholarship and Fellowship Plan. These cover travel to and from Australia, fees, living allowance and other expenses. Apply to Joint Secretaries, Commonwealth Scholarship Commission, Association of Commonwealth Universities, 36 Gordon Square, London WC1 0PE. For details of other grants, see: *Scholarships Guide for Commonwealth Postgraduate Students* (available in university and public libraries); *Awards for Postgraduate Study and Grants for Research in Australia* (Graduate Careers Council of Australia Ltd, PO Box 28, Parkville, Victoria, Australia 3052); and *Study Abroad* (UNESCO).

Joint programmes/special schemes
Commonwealth Scholarship and Fellowship plan.
Commonwealth Youth Exchanges (see p.51-52).

Other useful addresses
Australia Tourist Commission, Heathcote House, 20 Savile Row, London W1. Tel (01) 434 4371.

Student travel
Australian Union of Students Student Travel, 117 Euston Road,

London NW1. Tel (01) 388 2261.

SSA (STA), 17 Grattan Street, Carlton, Melbourne 3053, Victoria.

Australia's States
London offices for enquiries concerning particular States:
Victoria: Victoria House, Melbourne Place, London WC2. Tel (01) 836 2656.
Queensland: 392 Strand, London WC2. Tel (01) 836 3224.
South Australia: 50 Strand, London WC2. Tel (01) 930 7471.
Western Australia: 115 The Strand, London WC2. Tel (01) 240 2881.
New South Wales: 56 The Strand, London WC2. Tel (01) 839 6651.

BANGLADESH

Best areas of study Bengali, Sanskrit, Persian.
Language of tuition Bengali and English.
Academic Year January to December.
Best contacts for information
- University of Dacca, Ramna, Dacca 2.
- High Commission for the People's Republic of Bangladesh, 28 Queen's Gate, London SW7 5JA. Tel (01) 584 0081-4.

CANADA

See also introductory section on studying in the Commonwealth, p.51-52.

There are 50 universities in Canada, all of which take foreign students at undergraduate and postgraduate levels.

Language of tuition English in all universities except Laval, Moncton, Montreal, Quebec and Sherbrooke, which use French. At Ottawa and the Laurentian University of Sudbury both languages are used.

Academic year September to April.
Best contacts for information
- Association of Commonwealth Universities (ACU), 36 Gordon Square, London WC1H 0PF. Tel (01) 387 8572.
- Canadian High Commission, Canada House, Trafalgar Square, London SW1Y 5BJ. Tel (01) 629 9492.
- Association of Universities and Colleges of Canada (AUCC), 151 Slater, Ottawa, Ontario, Canada K1P 5N1.

1st degree courses

Foreign students are accepted on most degree courses except the 'co-operative programmes' (similar to UK sandwich courses) which involve periods spent in industry. Priority is given to Canadian students for places on professional degree programmes (business, computing, law etc); for medicine and dentistry the competition is so intense that foreign students are virtually excluded.

For general information on how to apply, see *Taking a First Degree at a Candian University* (information sheet available from the ACU — see above); and *University Study in Canada,* a booklet which also gives background information on life in Canada — accommodation, transport, welfare and so forth. Available from Canada House, see above.

Length Three years minimum; four years for Honours courses.

Contact

The Director of Admissions at each university. An address list can be obtained from Canada House (see above). To choose which universities to apply to, consult the *Commonwealth Universities Yearbook* or the *Directory of Canadian Universities,* available for consultation at Canada House, the ACU Reference Library (make an appointment first on (01) 387 8572), or other public or university libraries. The ACU library also holds prospectuses for reference purposes.

Entrance requirements

Two A levels and five GCSEs plus near native command of the language of tuition (English or French).

Cost/grants

Costs vary widely; some universities charge higher fees for foreign students. At time of writing the ACU reckons a year's undergraduate study could cost between $9,000 and $17,000, including accommodation and living costs. For up-to-date estimates contact the universities directly. Students would have to be self-financing as no grants are available for first degrees.

Postgraduate

Both Master's and Doctoral degrees usually include some course work as well as research. Not all universities offer research facilities for doctorates. See the publications mentioned above and also the

ACU leaflet *Graduate Study at Canadian Universities..*

Contact
The universities concerned; Canada House can provide on request a list of those offering your subject at postgraduate level.

Entrance requirements Good Bachelor's degree.

Grants
Awards covering the cost of travel, tuition and maintenance for one or two years are available under the Commonwealth Scholarship and Fellowship Scheme. Apply to the Joint Secretaries, Commonwealth Scholarship Commission, Association of Commonwealth Universities, 36 Gordon Square, London WC1 0PF.
    For details of other awards see the following publications:
Scholarships Guide for Commonwealth Postgraduate Students (available in university libraries).
Canadian Directory of Awards for Graduate Study (AUCC — see above).
Study Abroad (UNESCO — see p.174).
Guide to Awards open to British Postgraduate Students for study in Canada (from Canada House).

Language courses in Canada
Most universities in the French sector run intensive language courses. For stays with French speaking families in Canada, and seminars in literature, culture (in French), contact Collège de Rivière du Loup, 80 rue Frontenac, Rivière du Loup, Quebec G5R 1S8. Tel 862 6903 ext 293.

Joint programmes/special schemes
Commonwealth Scholarship and Fellowship plan (see above).
Commonwealth Youth Exchanges (see p.51-52).

BUTEC (see p.70).
CAPTEC (see p.70).

Welfare
The Canadian Bureau for International Education, 85 Albert Street, 14th Floor, Ottawa, Ontario, operates a reception service for overseas students. In universities, a Foreign Student Adviser deals with questions such as health, insurance, and accommodation.

Other useful addresses
Visas: Canadian High Commission, Employment and Immigration Division, 38 Grosvenor Street, London W1X 0AA. Tel (01) 409 2071.

Tourist Office, c/o Canada House, Trafalgar Square, London SW1. Tel (01) 629 9492.

Canada Universal Travel Service, 52 Grosvenor Gardens, London SW1. Tel (01) 730 9476.

Student travel
AOSC, 44 St George Street, Toronto, M5S 2E4, Ontario.

Regional offices in London
Alberta: 1 Mount Street, London W1Y 5AA.
British Columbia: 1-3 Lower Regent Street, London SW1Y 4NS.
Nova Scotia: 14 Pall Mall, London SW1Y 5LU.
Ontario: 13 Charles II Street, London SW1Y 4QS.
Quebec: 59 Pall Mall, London SW1Y 5JH.
Saskatchewan: 21 Pall Mall, London SW1Y 5LP.

For Manitoba, New Brunswick, Northwest Territories, Prince Edward Island, Yukon, Newfoundland and Labrador refer to the Canadian High Commission.

CYPRUS

Language of tuition English/Greek.
Academic year September to June.
Best contacts for information
● Cyprus High Commission, 93 Park Street, London W1Y 4ET. Tel (01) 499 8272.

1st degree courses
The University College of Northern Cyprus operates an American degree programme in business management. Contact the Academic Dean, UCNC, Girne, N. Cyprus. Tel (010 905) 815 4710.

Postgraduate
Cyprus College of Art runs a seven month course in fine arts, painting and sculpture, open to art graduates from any country. Some scholarships may be available, and accommodation is offered free. Contact Mr Stass Paraskos, 23 Oakwood Road, Sturry, Kent.

GHANA

Ghana has a more developed education system than many Commonwealth countries. The Association of African Universities is based in its capital, Accra.

Best areas of study African studies.
Language of tuition English.
Academic year October to June.
Best contacts for information
- Dean of Students, University of Ghana, Legon.
- Registrar, University of Cape Coast, Cape Coast.
- University of Science and Technology, Kumasi.

Postgraduate
The University of Ghana Institute of African Studies, PO Box 73, Legon (Accra), offers MA and PhD courses in African Studies; these include African arts and music, literature, sociology, politics, economics and languages. Grants are available at postgraduate level through the Commonwealth Scholarship and Fellowship Scheme, see p.50.

Summer school
The Institute also runs, on demand, introductory vacation courses in African studies. Apply to the Administration Secretary at above address.

Useful addresses
Ghana High Commission, 13 Belgrave Square, London SW1. Tel (01) 235 4142.
Education Section, 38 Queens Gate, London SW7. Tel (01) 584 6311.
Ministry of Education, PO Box M45, Accra.
Association of African Universities, PO Box 5744, Accra-North.

GUYANA

Language of tuition English.
Academic year September to July.
Best contacts for information
- University of Guyana, PO Box 101110, Georgetown.
- Student Affairs Division, Ministry of Education, 21 Brickdam and Pollard Place, Georgetown.

- High Commission for Guyana, 3 Palace Court, Bayswater Road, London W2. Tel (01) 229 7684.

INDIA

Language of tuition Mainly English.
Academic year June/July to April/May.
Best contacts for information
- Office of the High Commission for India, Education and Science Dept, India House, Aldwych, London WC2 4NA. Tel (01) 836 8484.
- Association of Indian Universities, Deendayal Upadhaya Marg, New Delhi 110 002. The Association is responsible for 150 universities and 350 polytechnics, and acts as an information clearing house.
- Students Information Service Unit, Ministry of Education and Culture, Shastri Bhawan, New Delhi 110 001.

Postgraduate
Various Indian institutes and university departments run specialist postgraduate programmes, as listed in the UNESCO publication *Study Abroad,* which is worth consulting on this. Areas include management, industrial design, mining, population studies, languages, agriculture and medicine.

The Gujarat Vidyapith Peace Research Centre runs one year courses leading to Master's degrees in peace studies, Gandhian thought, science and non-violence etc. The courses are run in Gujarati and/or Hindi, but language tuition is available. Further details from the centre at Ashram Road, Ahmedabad 380 014.

Grants
Grants are available through the Commonwealth Scholarship and Fellowship Plan, see p.50. The following institutions can also be approached for funding:
Indian Council of Social Science Research, 35 Ferozeshah Road, New Delhi 110 001.
Indian Institute of Technology, Hauz Khas, New Delhi 110 016.
Indian Institute of Technology Kanpur, Kanpur, Uttar Pradesh 208 016.
Institute of Constitutional and Parliamentary Studies, 18 Vithalbhai Patel House, Rafi Marg, New Delhi 110 001.
University of Agricultural Sciences, Post Bag no 2477, Hebbal,

Bangalore, Karnataka, 560 024.

Language courses
The University of Pune, Ganeshkhind, Pune 7411007, Maharashtra, runs six month courses in Maharashtra culture and language, open to students from all countries who have completed their secondary education.

For courses in Hindi at various levels, contact the Central Institute of Hindi, Delhi Campus, Shri Aurobindo Ashram, New Delhi 110 016.

Useful Addresses
India Government Tourist Office, 7 Cork Street, London W1. Tel (01) 437 3677.

Student travel
STIC, Hotel Imperial, Janapath, New Delhi.

IRELAND

See also introductory section on studying in the EC, p.74.

There are two universities in the Republic of Ireland: the National University of Ireland with colleges in Dublin, Cork and Galway, and Dublin University (Trinity College), and other institutions of higher education in Limerick and Dublin. They have a 7% foreign student population, about half of them British — either from Northern Ireland or other parts of the UK. Students from the UK do not need any special permits to enter or remain in the Republic.

Language of tuition English.
Academic year September/October to June/July.
Best contacts for information
● Central Applications Office, Tower House, Eglinton Street, Galway. Tel (091) 63318 (information about application and general information about courses).
● National University of Ireland, 49 Merrion Square, Dublin 2.
● Trinity College, University of Dublin, Dublin 1.
● See also: *Higher Education in the European Community,* a Student Handbook (see p.174).

1st degree courses (Bachelor's Degrees)
Length

Three years at National University of Ireland, four years at Trinity College.

Contact
Direct. See above for addresses. Applications through the Central Applications Office by 15th December.

Entrance requirements
Minimum of two A levels, plus at least good GCSE standard in English, another language, and Maths.

Cost/grants Fees vary according to subject and institution and are revised annally; expect to pay around £1,000 a year. Grants are not available unless your parents are resident in the Irish Republic.

Postgraduate (Master's or Doctoral Degrees)
Contact
The institutions directly. Contact the Registrar of each college in the case of the National University, or the Dean of Graduate Studies for Trinity College.

Entrance requirements Good Bachelor's degree.

Grants Costs are variable, but broadly similar to undergraduate fees. There are very few possibilities of grants, but try contacting:
● Department of Education, Marlborough Street, Dublin 1.
● Dublin Institute for Advanced Studies, 10 Burlington Road, Dublin 4.
● Royal Irish Academy, 19 Dawson Street, Dublin 2.

Visiting studentships
Possible at Trinity College for one year or one term, for students already undertaking a degree at another university. Apply directly to the University, not through the Central Applications Office.

Language courses
Five week Gaelic courses all the year round in Dublin, or two to three week residential courses in County Cork or County Donegal during the summer months are run by Foras Na Gaeilge, 26 Cearnóg Mhuirfean, Dublin 2. Tel (0001) 767 283.

Summer schools
A Celtic Studies Summer School is held every three years (1990,

1993), covering Irish language and literature, folklore, etc. Contact the Director, Dublin Institute for Advanced Studies, 10 Burlington Road, Dublin 4.

Summer Schools on Irish culture are also held at:

University College, Galway. Tel (010) 35391 24411.
University College, Dublin, Belfield, Dublin 4. Tel (0001) 693244.
Trinity College, Dublin University, Dublin 2. Tel (0001) 772941 ext 1177.

Welfare
Irish Council for Overseas Students, 41 Morehampton Road, Dublin.

Other useful addresses
Irish Embassy, 17 Grosvenor Place, London SW1X 7HR. Tel (01) 235 2171.
Irish Tourist Office, Ireland House, 150 New Bond Street, London W1Y 0AQ. Tel (01) 493 3201.
Department of Education, Marlborough Street, Dublin 1. Tel (0001) 717 101.
Higher Education Authority, 21 Fitzwilliam Square, Dublin 2. Tel (0001) 761 545.

Student travel
USIT, 7 Anglesea Street, Dublin 2.

JAMAICA

Language of tuition English.
Academic year September/October to June.
Best contacts for information.
- The Permanent Secretary, Ministry of Education, 2 National Heroes Circle, Kingston 4.
- Information Officer, University of West Indies, Mona, Kingston 6.

First degrees
See University of the West Indies, above. The Jamaica School of Art, 1 Arthur Wint Drive, Kingston 5, runs courses in painting, sculpture, textiles, jewellery, and ceramics based on Caribbean cultural traditions.

Postgraduate grants

Through the Commonwealth Scholarship and Fellowship Plan, see p.50.

Other useful addresses

Jamaican High Commission, 63 St James's Street, London SW1A 1LY. Tel (01) 499 8600.

Jamaica Tourist Board, 50 St James's Street, London SW1. Tel (01) 493 3647.

Student travel

JOYST, 9 Ripon Road, Kingston 5.

KENYA

Language of tuition English and Kiswahili.

Academic year September to June.

Best contacts for information

- Kenya High Commission, 45 Portland Place, London W1N 4AS. Tel (01) 636 2371.
- The Administrative Registrar, University of Nairobi, PO Box 30197, Nairobi.

Postgraduate

The British Institute in Eastern Africa, PO Box 30710, Nairobi, offers occasional research studentships and grants for postgraduate study into the pre-colonial history and archaeology of Eastern Africa. Contact the Director, at above address.

Special schemes

The National Museums of Kenya operate a Palaeoanthropological Field School for undergraduate students who spend six weeks at archaeological sites in Kenya. Apply to Koobi Fora Field School Program, PO Box 40658, Nairobi.

Useful Addresses

Ministry of Education, Science and Technology, PO Box 30040, Nairobi. Tel (010 2542) 28411.

MALAYSIA

Language of tuition Bahasa Malaysia, with some English.

Academic year May to January.

Useful addresses
Malaysian High Commission, 45 Belgrave Square, London SW1X
8QT. Tel (01) 235 8033.
Students Dept, 44 Bryanston Square, London W1H 8AJ. Tel (01)
723 2265.
University of Malaysia, Kuala Lumpur.
Malaysian Tourist Office, 17 Curzon Street, London W1Y 7FE. Tel
(01) 499 7388.

Student travel
MLS, 1st Floor, Southeast Asia Hotel, 69 Jalan Haji Hussein, Kuala
Lumpur.

NEW ZEALAND

See also introductory section on studying in the Commonwealth,
p.50-51.
 Opportunities for study in New Zealand are relatively few: there
are only six universities (plus one university college) and British
students are only accepted at postgraduate level.

Language of tuition English.
Academic year late Feb/early March to November.

Best contacts for information
- Association of Commonwealth Universities, 36 Gordon Square,
  London WC1. Tel (01) 387 8572. It produces a free Student In-
  formation paper entitled *Graduate Study at New Zealand
  Universities.*
- New Zealand High Commission, New Zealand House, 80
  Haymarket, London SW1Y 4TQ. Tel (01) 930 8422.

1st degree courses
Entry permits are not granted to British or Irish students wishing
to take first degree courses in New Zealand although some students
from South Pacific countries are accepted.

Postgraduate
Contact
For information on courses/specialised areas of research

available in each of the universities, consult in the first instance the *Commonwealth Universities Yearbook* in most university and many public libraries. For further information, write direct to the Universities concerned.

Entrance requirements
A good first degree in a relevant subject. Entry permits will not be granted if similar courses exist in the UK.

Grants
Grants are available under the Commonwealth Scholarship and Fellowship Plan to candidates under 35 with a good first degree. See ·p.50 for address for application. See also:
Scholarships Guide for Commonwealth Postgraduate Students, in libraries or from the ACU.
University Grants Committee, PO Box 12-348, Wellington North. Tuition and living expenses would be in the range NZ$8,000 to NZ$10,000 for self-supporting students.

Joint programmes/special schemes
Commonwealth Scholarship and Fellowship Plan.
Commonwealth Youth Exchanges.

Welfare
The New Zealand University Students' Association, PO Box 9047, Courtenay Place, Wellington, provides general assistance to students. It can supply free copies of *Overseas Students Handbook* which contains information on accommodation, living expenses etc. For further information on life in New Zealand, see also *Emigrating to New Zealand,* J. Thomas, T & L Publishing, 1983.

Other useful addresses
Ministry of Education, Director-General of Education, Private Bag, Wellington.
New Zealand Tours and Travel, 3 The Broadway, London N14. Tel (01) 882 0141.

Student travel
NZUSA, 22 Courtenay Place, Wellington.

NIGERIA

Language of tuition English.

Academic year October to June
Best contacts for information
- High Commission for the Federal Republic of Nigeria, Nigeria House, 9 Northumberland Avenue, London WC2N 5BX. Tel (01) 839 1244. Education and Consular Dept, 56-57 Fleet Street, London EC4Y 1BT. Tel (01) 353 3776.
- University of Ife, Ife, Nigeria. A number of postgraduate scholarships are available.
- The Nigerian Universities Office, 180 Tottenham Court Road, London W1 9LE. Tel (01) 637 4955. For information on study and research at Nigerian universities.

SINGAPORE

Best areas of study Full range. Of particular interest are the departments of Chinese, Malay and Japanese Studies.
Language of tuition English.
Academic year July to March.
Best contacts for information
- National University of Singapore, London Office, c/o Singapore High Commission, 5 Chesham Street, London SW1. Tel (01) 235 4562. Detailed information and a full range of booklets available.

1st degree courses
Length Three years minimum.
Contact National University of Singapore, as above.
Entrance requirements At least two A levels.
Cost/grants $3,000-$3,600 subsidised tuition fee for foreign students. More for dentistry and medicine. Loans available.

Postgraduate
Contact National University of Singapore, as above.
Grants Ask for the National University of Singapore booklet *Scholarships, Bursaries, Medals, Prizes, Loan Funds,* available through the London office.

Language courses
The University has a Chinese Language and Research Centre; this offers a range of courses, including an intensive three to four week course for foreigners — preferably graduates — wishing to gain pro-

ficiency in Chinese (Mandarin). Special courses can also be organised by arrangement. Contact the Chinese Language and Research Centre, National University of Singapore, Jurong Campus, Upper Jurong Road, Singapore 2263.

Other studies
The University also has a thriving Extra Mural Department, which runs a whole range of non-examined, non-certificated courses for all and sundry. Contact the Department of Extra Mural Studies, National University of Singapore, 13 Dalvey Estate, Singapore 1025.

Welfare
A Student Liaison Office (3rd Floor, Yusof Ishak House, Kent Ridge, Singapore 0511) looks after all aspects of student welfare, including accommodation, and gives advice and assistance to foreign students.

Other useful addresses
Information on courses offered by the two Polytechnics (Ngee Ann Polytechnic and Singapore Polytechnic) may be obtained from the Joint Admissions Board, Ministry of Education, Kay Siang Road, Singapore 1024.
Ministry of Education, Kay Siang Road, Singapore 1024.
Singapore Tourist Promotion Board, 1 Carrington House, 126 Regent Street, London W1. Tel (01) 437 0033.

SOUTH AFRICA

Education in South Africa is racially divided, with separate schools, colleges and universities for Whites, Blacks, Indians and Coloureds. 247,694 students were registered at South African universities in 1987, and of these only 61,678 were black.

Language of tuition English at the four English-speaking universities (Cape Town, Natal, Rhodes and Witwatersrand) and Afrikaans at the rest. Port Elizabeth University uses both.
Academic year March to November.
Best contacts for information
● South African Embassy, Trafalgar Square, London WC2N 5DP. Tel (01) 930 4488. It can supply a list of universities with their addresses. Almost all offer both postgraduate and first degree courses.

Language courses
For details of courses in Afrikaans, write to Dept of National Education, Vanderstelgebon, VanderStel Buildings, Private Bag, Pretoria 0001.

Other useful addresses
South African Universities Office, Chichester House, 278 High Holborn, London WC1V 7HE.

Student travel
SASTS Ltd, 202 Dunwell House, 35 Jorissen Street, Braamfontein 2001.

TANZANIA

Language of tuition English.
Academic year June to March.
Best contacts for information
● University of Dar-es-Salaam, PO Box 35091, Dar-es-Salaam.
● High Commission for the United Republic of Tanzania, 43 Hertford Street, London W1. Tel (01) 499 8951-4.

Language courses
Two and four week courses in Swahili for foreigners are run by the Institute of Kiswahili and Foreign Languages, PO Box 882, Zanzibar.

USA

A potentially bewildering number of possibilities exist for study in the USA. The education system is not centrally controlled in any way and there are over 3,000 state and private colleges and universities which almost all accept foreign students. Sources of funding exist, but you are likely to have to find at least half the costs of study from your own resources.

Language of tuition English.
Academic year September to May.
Best contacts for information
An essential first contact is the Fulbright Commission office in London which exists specifically to advise and inform foreign students on the possibilities of study in the USA:
● Educational Advisory Service (Fulbright Commission), 6 Porter

Street, London W1M 2HR. Tel (01) 486 1098 (hours 11 am to 4.30 pm).

1st degree courses

Length
Normally four years, but the credit system could allow you to finish in three by accepting A levels or other qualifications as 'advance standing' towards the degree.

Contact
The Educational Advisory Service, as above. They hold a good range of guides, directories and prospectuses of US colleges, and employ several full-time advisors to help you choose which ones to approach, taking into account such factors as cost, location, type of institution, academic standing, etc. They also have access to a computer-search facility which can help narrow down choices. Their leaflet *Applying to American Universities for Undergraduate Study* or the Fulbright Commission booklet *Undergraduate Study in the United States* give detailed information on how to apply. Applications should be made in the autumn ('fall') of the year before you wish to start.

Entrance requirements
Normally A levels, but some lesser institutions accept five *good* GCSEs in a range of subjects including English and Maths. There are also admission tests: many institutions accept the *Scholastic Aptitude Test* (SAT) which may be taken in the UK — see the Educational Advisory Service for details. If English is not your native language you will also have to sit a 'TOEFL' exam in this subject.

Cost/grants
Costs vary widely, but in general the state universities are cheaper than private ones. Living expenses are roughly similar to the UK, but also vary according to region — costs are highest in the big cities. The Educational Advisory Service can give you a leaflet *Awards for Undergraduate Study in the United States* which lists institutions offering (partial) financial aid to foreign students. In order to be granted a visa to enter the US, you will have to show evidence of being able to meet the full costs of tuition and living expenses throughout your stay.

Postgraduate

Contact
Educational Advisory Service, as above, asking initially for the information leaflets: *Postgraduate Study in the United States* and *Applying to American Universities for Postgraduate Study.* This office will also send, on request, a list of institutions offering your chosen subject at postgraduate level. Early application is recommended.

Entrance requirements
At least a 2.2 degree; a 2.1 is necessary to be eligible for financial aid. Other qualifications (eg HND) may be considered on an individual basis. Candidates must also sit a 3 ½ hour **Graduate Record Examination** designed to evaluate reasoning ability in English and Maths, plus an English language exam for non-native speakers, as above.

Grants
Finance may be available from the universities themselves or from independent foundations. Ask for the Educational Advisory Service leaflet *Awards for Postgraduate Study and Research in the United States,* and consult also UNESCO's *Study Abroad* for details for awards for specific subjects. Awards may take the form of Fellowships, which are outright grants, or Graduate Assistantships, which involve some form of commitment to the university on the part of the graduate (usually assisting with teaching or research). This can mean that the full number of credits towards a higher degree cannot be completed in the normal time and you may take longer than anticipated getting your degree.

Visiting studentships
These are a real possibility, but can only be arranged by writing directly to the institution concerned.

Joint programmes/special schemes

- BUTEC (British Universities Transatlantic Exchanges Committee), and
- CAPTEC (Colleges and Polytechnics Transatlantic Exchanges Committee). These organisations encourage staff and student interchange between the UK and USA and Canada. Both are

based c/o Central Bureau, Seymour Mews House, Seymour Mews, London W1H 9PE. Tel (01) 486 5101.
- The Fulbright Programme (Fulbright Commission), 6 Porter Street, London W1M 2HR. Tel (01) 486 1098. This is developing links and joint study programmes between UK and US universities.

High school exchange programmes
- ASSE, 6 Harcourt Street, London W1H 2BD. Tel (01) 724 0280.
- Council on International Education Exchange (CIEE), 205 East 42nd Street, New York, NY 10017. Tel (0101 212) 661 1414.

These organisations offer 16-18 year olds the chance to live with an American family and spend a year at an American High School.

Welfare
Every university/college has at least one Foreign Student Advisor to help and advise on such matters as immigration, registration, insurance, health, accommodation, and work permits for summer employment. There is also an **International Student Service Arrival Program** which meets foreign students when they arrive at the airport and can help you find temporary accommodation.

Other useful addresses
Visa Unit, American Embassy, 5 Upper Grosvenor Street, London W1. Tel (01) 499 3443.
US Travel and Tourism Administration, 22 Sackville Street, London W1. Tel (01) 439 7433.

Student travel
See CIEE above.

OTHER COMMONWEALTH COUNTRIES: CONTACT ADDRESSES

Antigua and Barbuda. High Commission for Antigua and Barbuda, Antigua House, 15 Thayer Street, London W1M 5DL. Tel (01) 486 7073-5.
Bahamas. High Commission for the Bahamas, 10 Chesterfield Street, London W1X 8AH. Tel (01) 930 6967-9.
Barbados. Barbados High Commission, 1 Great Russell Street, London WC1B 3NH. Tel (01) 361 4975.
Belize. Belize High Commission, 15 Thayer Street, London W1M

5DL. Tel (01) 486 8381.

Botswana. Botswana High Commission, 6 Stratford Place, London W1N 9AE. Tel (01) 499 0031. University of Botswana, Private Bag, 0022 Gaborone.

Dominica. Office of the High Commission for the Commonwealth of Dominica, 1 Collingham Gardens, London SW5. Tel (01) 370 5194.

Eastern Caribbean States (St Christopher and Nevis, St Lucia, St Vincent and the Grenadines). High Commission for the Eastern Caribbean States, 10 Kensington Court, London W8. Tel (01) 937 9522.

The Gambia. The Gambia High Commission, 57 Kensington Court, London W8 5DG. Tel (01) 937 6316.

Gibraltar. Dept of Education, 40 Town Range, Gibraltar.

Grenada. High Commission for Grenada, 1 Collingham Gardens, London SW5. Tel (01) 373 7808.

Lesotho. High Commission for the Kingdom of Lesotho, 10 Collingham Road, London SW5 0NR. Tel (01) 372 8581.

Malawi. High Commission for the Republic of Malawi, 33 Grosvenor Street, London W1X 0HS. Tel (01) 491 4172.

Mauritius. Mauritius High Commission, 32/33 Elvaston Place, London SW7. Tel (01) 581 0294-8.

Papua New Guinea. Papua New Guinea High Commission, 3rd Floor, 14 Waterloo Place, London SW1R 4AR. Tel (01) 930 922. Papua New Guinea University of Technology, Private Bag Mail, Lae, Morobi Province, Papua New Guinea.

Seychelles. High Commission for Seychelles, Box No. 4PE, 4th Floor, 50 Conduit Street, London W1A 4PE. Tel (01) 439 0405.

Sierra Leone. Sierre Leone High Commission, 33 Portland Place, London W1N 3AG. Tel (01) 636 6483.

Solomon Islands. Write to: The Permanent Secretary, Ministry of Foreign Affairs, PO Box G10, Honiara, Solomon Islands.

Swaziland. Kingdom of Swaziland High Commission, 58 Pont Street, London SW1 0AE. Tel (01) 581 4976-8.

Tonga. Tonga High Commission, 12th Floor, New Zealand House, Haymarket, London SW1Y. Tel (01) 839 3287-8.

Trinidad and Tobago. Office of the High Commission for the Republic of Trinidad and Tobago, 42 Belgrave Square, London SW1X 8NT. Tel (01) 245 9351.

Uganda. Uganda High Commission, Uganda House, 58-9 Trafalgar Square, London WC2N 5DX. Tel (01) 839 5783. Education Dept, 189 Wardour Street, London W1. Tel (01) 734 9718.

Zambia. High Commission for the Republic of Zambia, 2 Palace Gate, London W8 5LS. Tel (01) 589 6655.

Zimbabwe. Zimbabwe High Commission, Zimbabwe House, 429 Strand, London WC2R 0SA. Tel (01) 836 7755. The Secretary of Education, PO Box 8022, Causeway, Harare. University of Zimbabwe, PO Box MP 167, Mount Pleasant, Harare.

Europe

Studying in Europe has the great advantage that it is right on our doorstep — no long-distance travel is involved and communications are generally fast and frequent. In some cases travel is so easy that you can afford to visit and inspect the institution where you will be studying before you sign up for the course — a great advantage — and you can even pop home for the odd weekend.

STUDYING IN THE EUROPEAN COMMUNITY

The European Community's policy to promote freedom of access to education and training throughout the community has led to a great many opportunities for study abroad being opened up in recent years, and these are expanding all the time. They include the following variations:

- Following a course at an institution in another EC country (a vital resource here is *Higher Education in the European Community,* see p.174).
- Following a joint study course based at a UK institution, but which includes a period of study abroad (see p.21 and also *Joint Study Courses* — CRAC Degree Course Guides).
- A short exchange or visit within the context of a UK course (see p.22).
- A language course (see p.27).

For details of all EC schemes, see p.18-26.

EASTERN EUROPE

Following the recent dramatic political upheavals in Eastern Europe, this is perhaps the area of the world likely to see the greatest expansion of study opportunities in the next few years. For the moment opportunities for study in Eastern Europe are still rather restricted to special bilateral schemes administered through the **British Council,** especially the Specialist Tours Department (see below). British Council offices in the countries concerned can be a good source of information — some addresses are included on the following pages. A full list can be obtained from the British Council, 10 Spring Gardens, London SW1A 2BN. Tel (01) 930 8466.

Education in Eastern Europe has traditionally (at least since the establishment of communist/socialist states) been closely tied to the economic needs of the country, rather than seen as a means by which individuals can better their status or improve their minds. This naturally imposes limitations on opportunities for the independent student. However at the time of writing the tendency is towards a greater liberalisation and the next few years should see an opening up of opportunities for foreigners in at least some of these countries. It is to be hoped at least that none go the way of Albania where no discernible opportunities for foreigners exist at all.

USEFUL ADDRESSES

Great Britain-East Europe Centre, 31 Knightsbridge, London SW1X 7NH. Tel (01) 245 9771. This is an organisation which promotes greater understanding between the British and Bulgaria, Czechoslovakia, Hungary, Romania, Poland and East Germany. British Council, Specialist Tours Dept, 65 Davies Street, London W1Y 2AA. Tel (01) 499 8011.

Other European countries
In this section are included other countries which are our near neighbours and with which we therefore tend to have good relations, either through the Council of Europe or through bilateral schemes. Some good and varied opportunities exist in these countries.

AUSTRIA

Austria has 20 university level institutions, including four traditional universities: Vienna, Graz, Salzburg and Innsbruck.

Best areas of study Languages, Music.
Language of tuition German.
Academic year October to June.

Best contacts for information

- Austrian Institute, 28 Rutland Gate, London SW7 1PQ. Tel (01) 584 8653.
- Austrian Foreign Students Service, University of Vienna, Dr Karl Lueger-Ring (1/Stiege IX) A-1010 Vienna (also has offices in Innsbruck, Salzburg, Leoben and Klagenfurt).

1st degree courses
Entrance requirements
Evidence of having already been offered a place at a university in one's own country, plus a pass in a compulsory German language examination.

Cost Tuition approx £150.

Postgraduate
There are international postgraduate courses in various disciplines listed in UNESCO's *Study Abroad*. Otherwise contact directly the institution where you wish to study.

Grants
The Austrian Government (Ministry of Science and Research) offers scholarships to British graduates for one academic year's study or research at any Austrian university level institution. Good German is essential. Apply to the Austrian Institute, 28 Rutland Gate, London SW7 1PQ. Tel (01) 584 8653, by January or February each year. There are also grants for one month's independent research in libraries, archives etc, or for attending summer schools (see below). Conditions and application procedures as above.

Summer schools
The Austrian Institute in London (see above) can supply a booklet published each year entitled *Summer Courses in Austria;* one month bursaries are available for attending these (see above). They include language and music courses at a number of institutions. For instance:

The University of Vienna Summer School includes German language, Austrian culture and history and international politics, mountain walking and excursions. Applicants must have completed one year of a university course. Contact address: University of Vienna, Summer School Office, Wahringerstrasse 17, 1090 Vienna. Tel (01043 222) 436 141 ext 60.

The International Summer Academy, Mirabellplatz 1, 5020 Salzburg, runs courses in conducting, opera singing, chamber music, flute, clarinet etc.

Holiday music courses in Tyrolean Alpine village: Berwang Holiday Music Courses, The Secretary, Willowdown, Megg Lane, Chipperfield, Herts, WD4 9JN. Tel (09277) 63715.

Language courses

German
Of particular interest are the courses run as summer courses and throughout the year in Salzburg and elsewhere by Internationale Ferienkurse für Deutsche Spache und Germanistik, Franz-Josef Strasse 19, A-5020 Salzburg.

The Anglo-Austrian Society, 46 Queen Anne's Gate, London SW1H 9AU, tel (01) 222 0366, handles applications and travel arrangements for German language courses at a range of institutions in Austria, including an Easter holiday course for GCSE and A level students.

Osterreichische Vereinigung für Austausch und Studienreisen (OVAST) can arrange exchanges and holiday language courses for students aged 10-20.

Many other courses, for contacting directly, are listed in *Study Holidays*, published by Central Bureau (p.171).

You can also book courses through: Cultural and Educational Services Abroad (see p.28).

Czech, Hungarian, Russian
Intensive summer courses in these languages are run by Gesellschaft Für Ost Und Sudostkunde, Bismarkstrasse 5, A-4020 Linz. Tel (010 43732) 27 33 80.

Serbo-Croatian, Hungarian
Students with some prior knowledge of these languages can attend summer language courses organised by: Ostakademie, Ost-und Sudost Europa-Institut, Josefsplatz, A-1010 Vienna. Tel (010 43222) 512 1895.

Other useful addresses
Austrian National Tourist Office, 30 St George Street, London W1R 9FA. Tel (01) 629 0461.

Austrian Embassy, 18 Belgrave Mews West, London SW1X 8HU. Tel (01) 235 3731.

Student travel
BfSt, Schreyvogelgasse 3, A-1010 Vienna.
OKISTA, Türkenstrasse 4, A-1090 Vienna.

BELGIUM

Belgian education is divided into two language sectors (French and Flemish), although both are organised under the same system. There are 17 degree giving institutions — 6 of them universities proper; the rest mainly offering specific professional qualifications.

Language of tuition French; Dutch (depending on institution).
Academic year October to July.
Best contacts for information
● Belgian Embassy, 103 Eaton Square, London SW1W 9AB. Tel (01) 235 5422 ext. 212.

1st degree courses

Length
Two to three years for the initial *candidat/kandidaat* qualification, and a further two to three years for the full *licencié/licentiaat*.

Contact
Institution of your choice. Applications should normally be received by 1st May to start the following October. Lists of universities are available from the Belgian Embassy, see above, or contained in *Higher Education in the European Community* (p.174).

Entrance requirements
French sector: 'A' levels or equivalent. Original certificate plus French translations of same, both legalised by the Belgian Embassy, must be sent to the university at time of application. You must also obtain a certificate from the Embassy of your proficiency in French.

Dutch sector
Determined by the university, although for degrees which prepare for a profession it's not possible to obtain the legal diploma to prac-tise unless secondary qualifications (ie A levels) have been recognised by the Belgisch Ministerie van Onderwijs, Bestuur van het Secundair onderwijs, Koningstraat 138, B-1000 Brussels.
 For further information on equivalencies, contact *Service des*

*équivalences de l'administration de l'enseignement secondaire/Dienst
gelijkwaardigheden van het bestuur van het secundair onderwijs*
(according to which sector you are applying to), Cité administrative
de l'Etat, bloc Arcades D, B-1010 Brussels. Tel (010 02) 564 8211.

Cost
Basic fees are £250 per year approx, but some categories of foreign
student may have to pay high extra foreign student fees, depending
on subject. Contact the university as soon as possible for exact details
pertaining to your particular situation.

Postgraduate

Contact Institution of your choice, as above.

Entrance requirements
To be admitted you must submit all documentation as for first degree
courses, plus official certification of studies undertaken during each
year of university education. For information on recognition of
university level studies, contact *Service des équivalences de l'enseignement superieur/Dienst gelijkwaardigheden van het bestuur van het
hoger onderwijs* of the Ministry of Education.

Grants
A number of postgraduate scholarships are offered each year through
the Belgian Embassy, Cultural Dept, 103 Eaton Square, London
SW1W 9AB. Tel (01) 235 5422. For awards for study in the French
community a working knowledge of French is required. The scholarships are for three to nine months only. *Study Abroad* (UNESCO)
lists various other grant-giving institutions for specific studies. There
are also special research grants for work on any aspect of European
Studies at the Free University of Brussels, Institut d'Etudes Euro-
péennes, 39 ave F.D. Roosevelt, B-1050 Brussels. Apply to the
Belgian Embassy for further information.

Language Courses in Belgium
Courses in both French and Dutch are available through both public
and private institutions, during summer and throughout the year.
The Belgian Embassy can supply contact addresses in addition to
those given below. **Bursaries** are available, through the Embassy,
for the following summer courses:

● French Language & Literature (four week courses), Free Univer-

sity of Brussels, 50 ave F.D. Roosevelt, B-1050 Brussels.
● Dutch Language & Culture (two week courses in Hasselt for students with some prior knowledge), Ministerie van de Vlaamse Gemeenschap, Administratie voor Onderwijszaken, Internationale Samenwerking, Kunstiaan 43, B-1040 Brussels. Tel (010 322) 513 74 64.

Other language courses

French courses for all levels throughout the year: Alliance Française de Bruxelles, 6 place Quételet, B-1030 Brussels. Tel (010 322) 218 25 66.

Five month French language courses: Athénée Royal de Maurice Careme-Wavre, Centre audio-visual de langue française, ave Henri Lepage, B-1300 Wavre.

Four year degree level courses in Translating and Interpreting: Institut Supérieur de l'État de Traducteurs et Interprètes, 34 rue Joseph-Hazard, B-1180 Brussels.

Dutch: Institute of Modern Languages and Communication, ave de la Toison d'Or 20, Brussels. Tel (010 322) 512 66 07.

Centre Linguistique de Thieusies, rue du Chateau 26, B-7461 Thieusies. Tel (010 3265) 72 84 90.

International College of Europe, Bruges.

Summer courses

The University of Peace at Namur, 4 Boulevard du Nord, B-5000 Namur. Tel (010 3281) 22 61 02. Runs a two week international summer course on peace studies, and weekend sessions throughout the year.

Bursaries are available through the Belgian Embassy for attendance at:
— International Arthur Grumiaux master class at Namur.
— Interpretation of Historical Musical Instruments, Antwerp.
— International Opera course, Alden Bieren.
— International Guitar Happening, Hasselt.
For further details apply to the Embassy.

Other useful addresses

Belgian National Tourist Office, 38 Dover Street, London W1X 3RB. Tel (01) 499 5379.

Ministry of Education (Dutch speaking), Rijksadminstratief Centrum, Arcadengebouw, 5 ver Dieping, B-1010 Brussels. Tel (010 322) 564 8211.

Ministry of Education (French speaking), Cité Administrative de l'Etat, boulevard Pachéco, B-1010 Bruxelles. Tel (010 322) 564 8211. College of Europe, UK Committee for the College of Europe, UACES Secretariat, King's College, Strand, London WC2R 2LS. Offers a one year course leading to the Diploma of Advanced European Studies to EC graduates in law, economics or political science.

BULGARIA

Bulgaria offers few possibilities except on officially approved schemes, as detailed below.

Language of tuition Bulgarian.
Academic year September to July.
Best contacts for information
- Ministry of National Education, Tchapaev St 55a, Sofia.
- Embassy of the People's Republic of Bulgaria, 186-188 Queens Gate, London SW7 5HL. Tel (01) 584 9400/9433.

Postgraduate
Approximately six research/study scholarships are offered each year to British students. Some knowledge of Bulgarian (or another Slavonic language) is expected. Apply through any British Council office.

Language courses
Summer school courses in Bulgarian language and culture are held each year in Sofia and in Veliko Turnovo. Approximately ten grants (not including travel expenses) are available each year for British students. Apply to Specialist Tours Dept, British Council, 65 Davies Street, London W1Y 2AA, tel (01) 499 8011.

Useful addresses
Bulgarian National Tourist Office, 18 Princes Street, London W1R 7RE. Tel (01) 499 6988.

Student travel
BMT, 45a Stambouliiski Boulevard, Sofia.

CZECHOSLOVAKIA

Czechoslovakia has strong educational traditions. The Charles

University of Prague was the first in Central Europe (founded in 1348) and the great seventeenth century educational reformer Comenius was a Czech. Today there are two Ministries of Education, Czech and Slovak, which are responsible for a unified educational policy.

Language of tuition Czech and Slovak, depending on which Socialist Republic you're in.

Academic year September to August.

Best contacts for information
● British Council, 65 Davies Street, London W1Y 2AA. Tel (01) 499 8011. See also their publication *Scholarships Abroad*.

Postgraduate

About seven postgraduate scholarships are available each year for British graduates with some knowledge of Czech or Slovak. These last ten months, through Cultural Exchange Programmes administered by the British Council. Apply to the Overseas Educational Appointments Department of the British Council, address as above, by mid November each year.

There are certain specialist postgraduate courses — mostly in scientific fields — open to foreign nationals and held in English. A full list is contained in UNESCO's *Study Abroad*.

Visiting studentships

Bursaries are availble for two week and two month working/study visits, arranged through the British Council, but generally only for established academics. Apply to the Specialist Tours Dept of the British Council, as above.

Language courses

Summer schools for advanced students of Slavonic studies are held each year at the Charles University of Prague and the Comenius University of Bratislava:

● Universitas Carolina Pragensis, Letní Skola Slovanskych Studií, Filozoficka Fakulta UK, nám. Krasnoarmejcu 2, 116 38 Praha 1.
● Studia Academica Slovaca, Filozofická Fakulta, Univerzita Komenského, Gondova 2, 806 01 Bratislava.

Courses in Czech language are held at:

● Letrií Skola Slovanskych Studií, Filozofická Fakulta University J E Purkyne v Brne, Arna Nováka 1, 602 00 Brno.

Bursaries are available to British students wishing to attend these courses; apply through the Specialist Tours Dept, British Council, as above.

Other useful addresses
Embassy of the Czechoslovak Socialist Republic, 25 Kensington Palace Gardens, London W8 4QY. Tel (01) 229 1255.
Ministry of Education of the Czech Socialist Republic, Prague.
Ministry of Education of the Slovak Socialist Republic, Bratislava.
CEDOK (Czechoslovak Tourist Office), 17-18 Old Bond Street, London W1X 3DA. Tel (01) 629 6058.

Student travel
CKM, 12 Zitna Ulice, 121 05 Prague 2.

DENMARK

Denmark has three traditional universities, two new *universitets-centre,* and various other colleges. Knowledge of Danish is generally a key factor in taking advantage of study opportunities offered.

Language of tuition Danish.
Academic year September to June.
Best contacts for information
● In the first instance, the Royal Danish Embassy, 55 Sloane Street, London SW1X 9SR. Tel (01) 235 1255.

1st degree courses
Length Varies, but generally much longer than UK degrees.

Contact
Universities or colleges concerned. See first the factsheet distributed by the Danish Embassy in London entitled *Studying in Denmark,* which includes useful general information and a list of addresses.

Entrance requirements
At least two 'A' levels, plus a good working knowledge of Danish, which is generally subject to a test by the institution concerned. There are a number of degrees, including especially medically-related subjects, for which foreign students are not accepted unless they have special ties with Denmark. Closing date for applications is 15th March to start the following September.

Cost/grants
Tuition is free. Maintenance grants are not usually payable to foreign students for first degree courses, although EC nationals are not prohibited from working.

Postgraduate

Contact Universities concerned.

Entrance requirements
A Bachelor's degree, plus good working knowledge of Danish for taught courses. Individual researchers may be able to get by without it.

Grants
(a) Danish Government Scholarships for eight months or less, apply through Danish Embassy.
(b) Anglo-Danish Society Scholarships for six months or less, apply direct to: Anglo-Danish Society, 7 St Helen's Place, London EC3A 6BH.

Visiting studentships

Facilities are available for foreign students to enrol as guest students in Danish universities for one or two terms, but without actually having to complete any specific courses of study. Knowledge of Danish is required, but is not usually tested prior to admission. Apply direct to the institution concerned. The **Information Centre for Study and Exchange Programmes** (ICU), Bremerholm 6, 4th floor, DK-1069 Copenhagen K, tel (010 451) 911 515, will give free advice to individuals or groups wishing to visit Denmark for this and other educational purposes.

Language courses

The Studieskolen of Copenhagen University (Antonigade 6, DK-1106 Copenhagen K) runs special subsidised language courses for foreign students intending to take courses at Danish universities. The Danish Embassy in London can supply lists of institutions, mainly in Copenhagen, offering short term or summer Danish language courses. For information see also:
- Folk High School Information Office, Vartov Opgang 6, Favergade 27, DK-1463 Copenhagen K. Tel (010 451) 13 98 22.
- Det Danske Selskab, Kultorvet 2, DK-1175 Copenhagen K. Tel

(010 451) 13 54 48.

Folk High Schools
The Folk High School is a peculiarly Danish institution which provides adult education through study circles, discussions, project groups etc as well as more traditional means. There are over 100 Folk High Schools throughout Denmark; information on the courses being run may be obtained from the Folk High School Information Office, Vartov Opgang 6, Favergade 27, DK-1463 Copenhagen K. Tel (010 451) 13 98 22.

Joint programmes/special schemes
A special International Study Programme is held at the University of Copenhagen (in English) each year, attracting English-speaking undergraduates from all over the world, especially USA, Canada and Australia. Courses are run in liberal arts, business studies, architecture and design and last either three or four months, or a whole academic year. Scholarships are available. A publication entitled *Holiday Courses for Students and Visitors from Abroad* gives full details and can be obtained from: DIS Study, University of Copenhagen, Vestergade 9, DK-1456 Copenhagen.

The Nordenfjord World University, New Experimental College, Sykum Bjerge, 7752 Snedsted THY, runs a variety of courses on themes relating to 'world education', lasting from three to nine months. Seminars are held in English and bursaries are available.

Det Danske Selskab, Kultorvet 2, DK-1175 Copenhagen K. Tel (010 451) 13 54 48. This is an organisation dependent on the Danish Ministry for Cultural Affairs which offers seminars, in English, on aspects of Danish Education and culture.

Specialised courses in architecture, interpreting, political science and other subjects are listed in *Study Abroad* (see p.174).

About eight joint study programmes with UK universities are in operation under the ERASMUS scheme.

Welfare
Accommodation in Copenhagen is difficult to find and expensive. The Danish Embassy's Factsheet includes a list of organisations which can help with student welfare, including the International Student Centres in Copenhagen (Dronningens Tvaergade 4, DK-1302 Copenhagen K) and Arhus (Niels Juelsgade 84, DK-8200 Arhus N).

Other useful addresses
● Ministry of Education, International Office, Frederiksholms

Kanal 21, DK-1200 Copenhagen K. Tel (010 451) 925 000.
● The Danish Cultural Institute, 3 Doune Terrace, Edinburgh EH3 6DY. Tel (031) 225 7189.
● Danish Tourist Board, Sceptre House, 169-173 Regent Street, London W1R 8PY. Tel (01) 734 2637.

Student travel
DIS, 28 Skindergade, DK-1159 Copenhagen K.
SSTS, Hauchsvej 17, DK-1825 Copenhagen K.

FINLAND

Finland has 20 university institutions, by far the largest and most ancient of which is the University of Helsinki. There are good opportunities for those interested in learning the Finnish language.

Language of tuition Finnish and Swedish.
Academic year September to May.
Best contacts for information
● Embassy of Finland, 38 Chesham Place, London SW1X 8HW. Tel (01) 235 9531.

1st degree courses
Length Four years or longer.

Contact
The Finnish Embassy can supply a comprehensive booklet entitled *Higher Education in Finland: Guide for Foreign Students.* This gives general information or organisation of universities, degrees, grants and loans, accommodation and welfare, student organisations, and so on; it also has detailed specific information relating to each university, its address, locations, courses offered, how to apply, specific entrance requirements, etc.

Entrance requirements
Generally two or three good 'A' levels and three other subjects at GCSE. A knowledge of French and/or Swedish (depending on the faculty to which you are applying) is also necessary, and there is an entrance examination in most cases as well.

Cost
Tuition is free. Grants and loans are available for students regarded

as being ordinarily resident in Finland. Apply directly to: Valtion Opintotukikeskus, Vapaudenkatu 48-50, PL 228, SF-40101, Jyväskylä 10. Tel (010 35841) 215 611.

Postgraduate

Contact The universities themselves, see above.

Entrance requirements
Master's degree. The authorities suggest you may be able to get by without knowing Finnish or Swedish for some postgraduate work.

Grants
The Finnish Government offers scholarships to British graduates for study in Finland for up to nine months. Knowledge of Finnish 'useful but not essential'. Apply through the Finnish Embassy in London (see above), by January.

The Finnish Ministry of Education offers nine-month scholarships for advanced studies in Finnish language or culture, usually to students who already have a degree in Finnish studies. There are also Postdoctoral Specialist Scholarships for shorter periods. Apply directly to the Ministry of Education, Department for International Relations, Scholarship Centre, Vuorikatu 8 A 7, SF-00100, Helsinki, tel (010 3580) 171 636, or to the Finnish Embassy for further details.

Language courses
Finnish for foreigners courses are run by several of the universities, notably Helsinki, for which you should apply to: The Secretary, Suomen Kielen Ulkomaalaisopetus, Helsingin Yliopisto, Fabianinkatu 33, SF-00170 Helsinki. Further details appear in the *Higher Education in Finland* booklet referred to above.

There are also Summer Courses in Finnish as a foreign language, run at various centres by the Ministry of Education. Details of these are published annually by the Council for Instruction of Finnish for Foreigners, Vuorikatu 5 B 18, SF-00100, Helsinki 10. Tel (010 3580) 629 470. Other sources of information on these courses are:
- Ministry of Education, Department for International Relations (see above).
- *Finnish Courses,* a newsheet put out jointly by the Finnish Embassy and the University of London School of Slavonic and East European Studies (it also lists Finnish courses in the UK).
- *Study Abroad* (see p.174).

Joint programmes
IAESTE (see p.23). Also, an Anglo-Finnish Summer School is held each year in an attractive part of Finland, bringing together both Finns and Brits in a study-holiday type atmosphere. For further details apply to: Toyrytie IAI, 33530 Tampere 53, Finland.

Useful addresses
Finnish Tourist Board, 66-68 Haymarket, London SW1Y 4RF. Tel (01) 839 4048.

Student travel
FSTS, Mannerheimintie 5C, SF-00100 Helsinki 10.

FRANCE

France has more than 200 higher education institutions, including 72 traditional universities. They include the various *écoles* or *grandes écoles* which are not linked to the Ministry of Education and which select students by means of very tough competitive examinations. In addition France has very well developed facilities for promoting French language and culture, and courses of this nature abound.

Language of tuition French.
Academic year October to June.
Best contacts for information
● French Embassy Cultural Section, 22 Wilton Crescent, London SW1X 8SB. Tel (01) 235 8080.

1st degree courses
Length Two years for Diploma *(DEUG),* three for *licence,* four for *maîtrise.*

Contact
Ministère de l'Education Nationale, Direction de L'Enseignement Supérieur, Bureau d'information et d'orientation, 61/65 rue Dutot, 75015 Paris. Tel (010 331) 539 2575 ext 32-79 and 37-47. This is the Ministry of Education information bureau in charge of higher education.
    L'Office Nationale d'Information sur les Enseignements et les Professions (ONISEP), 168 boulevard de Montparnasse, 75014 Paris. Has a range of publications for sale and consultation on careers and university studies.

Applications
You should apply for university places in December and January each year (final deadline 1st February), on forms available from the French Embassy Cultural Section.

Entrance requirements
Minimum two 'A' levels and three GCSEs, or other equivalent of the French baccalaureate. There are no entrance exams. Knowledge of French is required; this can be brought to an acceptable level by attending a course specially laid on for this purpose before the beginning of the academic year (see Language Courses below). Tests can be taken either in the UK (apply to French Embassy Cultural Section, as above) or at the first university of your choice.

Cost/grants
Tuition costs are minimal: a total of approximately £80 should cover all tuition and registration fees.

Postgraduate
Postgraduate students coming from the British system would take either the one year *maîtrise* (see above) or a doctorate (three years), or a one year professional qualification *(DESS)*.

Contact
The universities themselves. Lists may be obtained from Ministry of Education or Embassy; see above.

Entrance requirements Minimum requirement is a good Bachelor's degree.

Grants
For French Government scholarships in the Arts (French language and culture, and performance arts) contact Service Culturel, 22 Wilton Crescent, as above. For French Government scholarships in scientific fields (applied biotechnology, materials science and composites and microelectronics only), contact Scientific Counsellor, French Embassy, Silver City House, 62 Brompton Road, London SW3 1BW. In both cases applications must be made by mid January, through your university department if you are currently studying in the UK.
  Research fellowships and short-term research bursaries in science or humanities are offered to British postgraduates *with some research*

experience by the *Centre National de la Rescherche Scientifique*. Apply to British Council, OEAD, 65 Davies Street, London W1Y 2AA, by March.

Scholarships for French studies are offered by the British Institute in Paris. Apply to the Secretary, British Institute in Paris, Senate House, Malet Street, London WCH 7HU.

Exchange fellowships in the field of biomedical research: apply to the Training Awards Group, Medical Research Council, 20 Park Crescent, London W1N 4AL.

The *Centre Nationale des Oeuvres Universitaires et Scolaires* (CNOUS), 69 Quai d'Orsay, 75007 Paris, has special responsibility for foreign students and grants open to them in France.

Visiting studentships in France
Contact CROUS (Centres Régionaux des Oeuvres Universitaires et scolaires), 39 av Georges Bernanos, Paris 75005.

Language courses
The Service Culturel (see above) can send you a booklet entitled *Cours de Français pour étudiants étrangers*. It is published annually and lists French language courses up and down the country open to foreign students, including those run by or in conjunction with universities, and those offered by private organisations. The information given includes the type of course, its organisation, dates, costs and practical information on student life, as well as contact addresses. Courses range from language courses for complete beginners to university level courses leading to recognised diplomas; the wide choice means that you should be able to find a course to suit your exact requirements in terms of level, timing, and so forth. Specialist courses are run for students intending to start regular university courses in France, non-native teachers of French, and people needing French for special purposes. This information comes in French. Similar information in English is contained in *Study Holidays* published by the Central Bureau for Educational Visits and Exchanges (see p.171). A few examples are as follows:

Courses run by the **Alliance Française** — an important French teaching association with branches worldwide. See below for the address of the London branch. In France write to one of the following addresses:

1 rue Vernier, 0600 Nice. Tel (010 3393) 87 42 11.

101 boulevard Raspail, 75270 Paris. Tel (010 331) 45 44 38 28.
32 rue de Buffon, 76000 Rouen. Tel (010 3335) 98 55 99.
9 place du Capitole, 31000 Toulouse. Tel (010 3361) 23 41 24.

Courses are run by well known private language teaching organisations, such as **Eurocentres,** 13 passage Dauphine, 75006 Paris, tel (010 331) 43 25 81 40; 10 rue Amelot, 17000 La Rochelle, tel (010 33) 50 57 33; 1 avenue Léonard de Vinci, 37400 Amboise, tel (010 33) 23 10 60. **Inlingua,** 109 rue de l'Université, 75007 Paris, tel (010 331 45) 51 46 60; 8 rue de Coëtguen, Place de la Mairie, 35000 Rennes, tel (010 33) 51 46 60. There are many other private language schools much too numerous to list.

UK offices for French language courses
Some schools have offices or agents in the UK through which you can book courses:

Institut Britannique de Paris, London Office, University of London, Senate House, Room 215, Malet Street, London WC1E 7HU. Tel (01) 636 8000 ext 3920.

Inlingua School of Languages, 8-10 Rotton Park Road, Edgbaston, Birmingham B16 9JJ. Tel (021) 454 0204.

Cultural and Educational Services Abroad; see p.28.

Eurocentres; see p.29.

Eurolanguage, Greyhound House, 23-24 George Street, Richmond, Surrey, TW9 1HY. Tel (01) 940 1087.

Youth Travels Abroad, 117 Wendell Road, London W12 9SD. Tel (01) 743 7966.

En Famille Agency (Overseas), Westbury House, Queens Lane, Arundel, West Sussex BN18 9JN. Tel Arundel 883266.

School Travel Service, 24 Colloden Road, Enfield, Middlesex EN2 8QD. Tel (01) 363 8202.

Scholatravel, 8 South Parade, Weston-super-Mare, BS23 1JN. Tel 29037.

French Government Tourist Office, Youth Travel Dept (see below).

Summer schools
Programmes of study in French language, literature, theatre, music, art and so forth are run by:

Academie Internationale d'Eté, 89 bis avenue Sainte-Marie, 94016 Sainte-Mande.

Cours Universitaire d'Eté Saint Malo, Université Haute Bretagne, 6 avenue Gaston Berger, 35043 Rennes. Tel (99) 54 99 55.

Joint programmes/special schemes
ERASMUS.

Welfare
Special travel concessions and student social security covering medical
expenses.

Other useful addresses

● French Government Tourist Office, 178 Piccadilly, London
W1V 0AL. Tel (01) 491 7622.
● Alliance Française, 6 Cromwell Place, London SW7 2JN. Tel
(01) 723 6439.
● Institut Français, 14 Cromwell Place, London SW7 2JR. Tel (01)
581 2701. Also in Edinburgh.
● Ministère de l'Education Nationale, 110 rue de Grenelle, 75357
Paris. Tel (010 331) 4550 1010.

Student travel
OTU, 137 boulevard St Michel, 75005 Paris.

GERMANY (DEMOCRATIC REPUBLIC — EAST)

Although not as fruitful as West Germany, there are plenty of opportunities for (self-financed) language courses and summer schools,
as well as funding for postgraduate study and research through
British Council cultural exchange schemes.

Best areas of study German language, science and technology.
Language of tuition German.
Academic year September to June.
Best contacts for information
● Embassy of the German Democratic Republic, 34 Belgrave
Square, London SW1X 8QB. Tel (01) 235 9941-3.

1st degree courses
On a self-financing basis only. Further details from the GDR
Embassy.

Postgraduate
The GDR government offers about four scholarships a year for
British postgraduates. Applicants should be under 35 and have a

good knowledge of German. The scholarships cover tuition, board and lodging for five or ten months. Apply through the British Council, 65 Davies Street, London W1Y 2AA, by mid November.

Language courses

The GDR Embassy can provide a booklet entitled *Intensive Courses in German as a Foreign Language;* it lists the general courses available each year, gives addresses, and includes an application form. Tuition for specialist language needs may be arranged with individual institutions. There is also a good list of courses in the relevant section of the Central Bureau's publication *Study Holidays.*

Bursaries are available for teachers and students of German wishing to attend language, literature or related studies summer schools in the GDR. Apply by February each year to the British Council Specialist Tours Dept.

Summer schools

As well as language courses, a wide range of International Summer Schools are held each year, open to all speakers of German. Ask the Embassy for their booklet *Internationale Hochschulferienkurse für Germanistik.*

Specialist courses

East Germany has a number of prestigious university institutions whose various faculties often run courses — in English — for specialists working in the field, usually science and technology. Best contacts are made through one's own institution, but a list is given in UNESCO's *Study Abroad.*

Other useful addresses

Student travel
JT, Alexanderplatz 5, 1026 Berlin.

GERMANY (FEDERAL REPUBLIC — WEST)

There are 238 university institutions in West Germany, including universities, specialist colleges and the relatively new *Fachhochschulen* (Polytechnics). It's a country with strong academic traditions and many 'centres of excellence' for research especially in scientific and technological fields. In addition the Goethe Institutes and many private language schools provide a wealth of opportunities for learning German language and culture.

Language of tuition German.
Academic year Divided into two semesters, starting in October and April.
Best contacts for information
● German Academic Exchange Service *(Deutscher Akademischer* Austauschdienst, DAAD), 17 Bloomsbury Square, London WC1A. Tel (01) 404 4065.
● DAAD Headquarters, Kennedyallee 50, D-5300 Bonn 2, and branches throughout the world.

1st degree courses
Studies at German universities are divided into two stages — the first consists of foundation studies after which an Intermediate Examination gives access to a second stage of more specialised studies. The degrees obtained after this second period are the *Magister Artium* (Arts and Humanities) and the *Diplom* (Social and Natural Sciences), which are normally regarded as equivalent to our Master's degrees.

Length
Most degree courses are scheduled to last about four years, but students have considerable freedom in choice of course components and present themselves for examination only when they think they are ready to take them, so it may take much longer than this to actually obtain the degree.

Contact
The **Akademische Auslandsämter** (Foreign Student Services) of each university. The DAAD (see above) can provide a booklet *Studies at Universities* which lists these, as well as providing detailed information about study in Germany.

Entrance requirements
The equivalent of the *Abiter* (ie 'A' levels) plus a very good knowledge of German. In some cases students are required to complete a preparatory course at a *Kolleg* — the DAAD can supply informtion on this. No formal qualifications are required for art and music colleges.

Cost/grants
Tuition is free, but living expenses — especially accommodation —

are high; no scholarships are generally available for foreigners for first degrees, so some means of support are necessary.

Postgraduate

Contact The Akademische Auslandsämter of each institution as above.

Entrance requirements
Usually a Master's degree in order to enrol for a doctorate (*Promotion* — the next degree after a *Magister* or *Diplom*) and, again, excellent German.

Grants
As with first degrees, tuition is free, but at postgraduate level various institutions offer grants for study and research. The DAAD booklet *Studies at Universities* (see above) lists an appendix of 'Institutions in the Federal Republic of Germany that provide Financial Aid to Foreign Students'.

The DAAD itself offers up to 15 postgraduate scholarships annually to British citizens with a good knowledge of German for study at German institutions in any field. It also offers short term (one to four months) research grants to PhD students or post-doctoral research workers. Apply through the DAAD office in London.

The Ministry of Education of the Rhineland-Palatinate offers one scholarship annually at the University of Mainz. Again British nationality and a good knowledge of German are essential. Apply through the British Council, Hahnenstrasse 6, D-5000 Cologne 1.

The Alexander von Humboldt Foundation offers a large number of post-doctoral fellowships to German speakers from all countries. Further information from Alexander von Humboldt-Stiftung, Jean-Paul-Strasse 12, D-5300 Bonn 2.

The King Edward VII British-German Foundation offers two or three postgraduate scholarships annually, tenable at any West German institution in any subject. Apply to The Secretary, King Edward VII British-German Foundation, 50 Hamilton Avenue, Pyford, Woking, Surrey GU22 8RU.

International University

The independent Schiller International University has a branch in Heidelberg, offering Bachelors and Masters degrees in liberal arts, European studies, economics, languages, business administration etc

— in English. For further details apply to Schiller International University, Friedrich-Ebert-Anlage 4, D-6900 Heidelberg.

Visiting studentships
Apply through the Akademisches Auslandsamt at each university.

Language courses
The Goethe-Instituts (16 in West Germany, 4 in the UK and a further 145 throughout the world) are universally recognized in the field of German as a Foreign Language. Their leaflet *Deutschlernen* gives full details of the many courses they run in Germany; it also includes an application form to be sent to their Head Office in Munich for central processing: Goethe-Institut, Lenbachplatz 3, D-8000 München 2. Tel (010 4989) 5999-200. There are Goethe-Instituts in Berlin, Bonn, Boppard, Bremen, Düsseldorf, Frankfurt, Freiburg, Göttingen, Iserlohn, Mannheim, Munich, Murnau, Prien, Rothenburg, Schwäbisch Hall and Staufen; central processing of applications means that if there are no places on your first choice of centre you can be assigned to another. For the leaflet mentioned above and any other queries, apply to one of the Goethe-Instituts in Britain:

50 Prince's Gate, Exhibition Road, London SW7 2PH. Tel (01) 581 3344.

Ridgefield House, 14 John Dalton Square, Manchester M2 6JR. Tel (061) 834 4635.

The King's Manor, Exhibition Square, York YO1 2EP. Tel (0904) 55222.

Scottish-German Centre, Lower Medway Building, 74 Victoria Crescent Road, Glasgow G12 9SC. Tel (041) 334 6116.

Language courses are also run by universities, partly as summer schools (see below) and partly for intending or current students who do not have German as a first language. In addition there are many private language schools big and small; details of these appear in the Central Bureau's guide *Study Holidays*. Large organizations such as Berlitz, Inlingua, Eurocentres and International House each have several centres. The organization Deutsch in Deutschland (head office Hauptstrasse 26, 8751 Stockstadt/Main, tel Stockstadt 20090) has 27 schools throughout the Federal Republic. Some courses may be booked through agents or offices in Britain (see p.28):

Cultural and Educational Services Abroad
Euro-Academy

Eurocentres
International House
International Study Programmes
School Journey Association, 48 Cavendish Road, London SW12
0DG. Tel (01) 673 4849.

See also the Organisation für Internationale Kontakte, Postfach
201051, D-5300 Bonn 2. Tel (010 49228) 357013.

Summer schools
The following institutions run International Summer Schools, each
lasting about a month, in German language, literature, culture and
society:

● Albert-Ludwigs University, Heinrich-von-Stephen-Strasse 25,
  D-7800 Freiburg im Breisgau.
● Christian-Albrechts University, Olshausenstrasse 40-60, D-2300
  Kiel.
● Trier University, Postfach 3825, D-5500 Trier.
● University of Bonn, Office for Foreign Academic Affairs,
  Nassestrasse 15, D-5300 Bonn.
● University of Munster, Schlossplatz 2, D-4400 Munster.
● University of Regensburg, Universitätstrasse 31, D-8400
  Regensburg.

There are also Musical Summer Schools (for music students or professional musicians) at the following:

● Musikalische Jugend Deutschland, Markplatz 12, D-6992
  Weikersheim.
● Internationales Musikinstitut Darmstadt, Nieder-Ramstädter
  Strasse 190, D-6100 Darmstadt.

Exchange Scholarships
Various German institutions offer Exchange Scholarships for
students enrolled at British universities (applications should generally
be made through the home university):

— Christian-Albrechts University, Olshausenstrasse 40-60, D-2300
  Kiel.
— Free University of Berlin, Altensteinstrasse 40, D-1000 Berlin 33.
— Ruprecht-Karls-Universität, Seminarstrasse 2, Postfach 105760,
  D-6900 Heidelberg 1 (with Universities of Cambridge and Sussex
  only).

— University of Bonn, Nassestrasse 15, D-5300 Bonn 1.

Welfare

All students have to pay a welfare contribution (between 20 and 60 marks per semester) to the Student Welfare Organisation **(Studentenwerk)** which covers the cost of the various services it provides. Health insurance is automatically covered for EC students.

Useful addresses

German National Tourist Office, 61 Conduit Street, London W1R 0EN. Tel (01) 734 2600.

Student travel

German Student Travel Service, Terminal House, Lower Belgrave Street, London SW1W 0NP. Tel (01) 730 2101.

ARTU, Hardenbergstrasse 9, D-1000 Berlin 12.

RDS, Rentselstrasse 16, D-2000 Hamburg 13.

Asta-Reisen, Keplerstrasse 17, K2 Stuttgart 1.

STR, Wilhelmstrasse 30, D-7400 Tübingen.

Federal Ministry for Education and Science, Heinemannstrasse 2, D-5300 Bonn 2.

GREECE

There is no private sector higher education in Greece — all institutions are financed and supervised by the state. These include nine universities (three of which were only created in 1984 and do not as yet offer the full range of courses), two polytechnics, and various other specialist colleges. Language courses are offered by both public and private sectors.

Language of tuition Greek.

Academic year October to June.

Best contacts for information

● Greek Embassy, 1a Holland Park, London W11. Tel (01) 727 8040.

● Ministry of Education, Section on Academic and Student Affairs (AEI), 15 Metropoleos Street, Athens.

1st degree courses

Length Minimum four years.

Contact
Institution of your choice. A list may be obtained from the Greek Embassy.

Entrance requirements
'A' levels. There is no entrance examination for non-Greek applicants, although knowledge of Greek may be tested. Application must be made *in person* to the Ministry of Education in July each year.

Cost
Tuition is free, although fees are payable by certain categories of foreign students (not generally from the EC). Board and lodging approx 35,000 drachmas per month.

Postgraduate
The organisation and duration of Greek postgraduate studies are undergoing reform, and at present considerable variation exists between faculties.

Contact Institution of your choice.
Entrance requirements Good first degree.

Grants
Ten 10-month scholarships for postgraduate work in a range of areas are offered each year by the Ministry of Education. Apply to the Greek Embassy by early April each year.

Scholarships for British students are offered by the University of Salonica, School of Modern Greek Language, Thessaloniki.

The John Augustus Saunders Memorial Fund offers scholarships for one academic year's study in a range of disciplines. Apply to OEAD, British Council, 65 Davies Street, London W1Y 2AA.

Grants for PhD work in any area of humanities are offered by the Foundation for State Bursaries, 14 Lysicrate Street, Athens; and by the Ministry of Education, Department of Higher Education, 15 Metropoleos Street, Athens.

Visiting studentships
The 'College Year in Athens' is designed mainly for US and Canadian students: by completing a year's study in Greece they can earn credit towards a degree in their own country. However the scheme is open to British students, too; a wide range of subjects relating to Greek

language and culture is on offer, together with visits to sites of interest. A prospectus is available from: College Year in Athens, PO Box 3476, Kolonaki, Athens. A similar, five month program(me) is offered by an organisation called Study in Greece. Their prospectus may be obtained from: Study in Greece, Neofronos 1, Athens 508.

Language courses
The Greek Embassy in London can supply a list of both state-run and privately organised courses in Modern Greek.

One year courses and summer courses are offered by the Athens University Club, 15 Hippokratous Street, Athens, tel (010 301) 3613261, and by the Aristotelian University of Thessaloniki School for Modern Greek Language, University Campus, Thessaloniki, tel (010 3031) 991381.

The Ionic Centre, 12 Stratiotikou Syndesmou Street, Athens, tel (010 301) 3604448, offers intensive courses in Modern Greek throughout the year, plus summer courses which take place on the island of Chios.

The Athens Centre for the Creative Arts, 48 Archimidous Street, Pangrati, Athens, tel (010 301) 701 5242, runs intensive part-time or summer courses in Modern Greek, with options in Greek dance, music, literature or history.

See *Study Holidays* (p.174) for details of other courses.

Summer schools
An international Summer School is organised each year by the Institute of Balkan Studies in Thessaloniki. Bursaries, and further information, are available through the Greek Embassy.

Joint programmes
At time of writing there are about ten ERASMUS schemes in operation with UK institutions.

Useful addresses
Students' Association/Athens University Club, 15 Hippokratous Street, Athens (information on accommodation etc).

The Anglo-Hellenic League, Room 1b, Chelsea College, Manresa Road, London SW3 6LX.

National Tourist Organisation of Greece, 195-197 Regent Street, London W1R 8DL. Tel (01) 734 5997.

Student travel
11 Nikis Street, 2nd Floor, Syntagma Square, 10557 Athens.

HOLLAND

Higher education in Holland, which is presently undergoing some reorganisation, is divided into two sectors. On the one hand, there is the purely academic sector comprising 13 universities and university colleges (*hogescholen*) plus 7 theological colleges; on the other hand there is the *hoger beroepsonderwijs* sector, which provides practical professional training in over 350 specialised institutions. Student numbers are split almost equally between the two sectors, although most foreign students find themselves in the academic sector, as residence permits are not usually given for the more practically-based courses. However Holland is strong on 'international education' — a whole range of relatively short duration courses at various institutions held in English. See below for further details.

Language of tuition Dutch.
Academic year October to June.
Best contacts for information
● Royal Netherlands Embassy, 38 Hyde Park Gate, London SW7 5DP. Tel (01) 584 5040.

1st degree courses

Length in academic sector
Four years, although students may take up to a maximum of six years to complete. The first year is a 'foundation year' and you must pass the **propaedeutisch examen** before passing on to the next stage.

Professional sector
Two to four years, depending on the type of studies undertaken.

Contact
The Ministry of Education and Science, Information Office, PO Box 25000, 2700 LZ Zoetermeer. Tel (010 31 79) 53 19 11. They can supply information about courses. Applications must be made through the **Central Bureau Aanmelding en Plaatsing** (CBAP), PO Box 888, 9700 AW Groningen, tel (0103150) 18 96 66, by 1st December each year.

Entrance requirements
Three 'A' levels and good Dutch. The authorities advise spending at least six months in the country learning the language before starting a degree course. See below for language courses.

Cost Approximately HFL1000. No grants are available.

Postgraduate
Second level professional university studies (**post-doctorate opleiding** — or graduate training) are not usually open to foreign students. However it's possible to do a doctoral degree in Holland and get special permission to write the thesis in English.

Contact
The Ministry of Education and Science, as above, or the universities themselves. A list is given in *Higher Education in the European Community* (see p.174) or in *Should You or Shouldn't You?,* a leaflet on studying in the Netherlands available from the Embassy in London. The following organizations can also help:

- VISUM, The Netherlands Information Centre for International Academic Mobility, PO Box 90734, 2509 LS The Hague, tel (010 31 70) 50 26 81.
- NUFFIC, Netherlands Universities Foundation for International Cooperation, Badhuisweg 251, 2509 LS, The Hague, tel (010 31 70) 57 42 01.

Entrance requirements Bachelor's or Master's degree.

Grants
A few nine month scholarships are available for British graduates. A knowledge of Dutch is 'desirable but not essential'. Apply through the Royal Netherlands Embassy by mid January each year.

Visiting studentships
Students can register as **toehoorders,** or guest students, although you still have to pay full fees. Contact NUFFIC, above, or the universities themselves.

International courses
There are 17 institutes in the Netherlands operating 'International Education' programmes. These were set up primarily for third world students but a large number of students from other countries attend. Courses, held in English, last from one month to two years, and

cover a wide range of subject areas: science and technology, social sciences, management studies, media and communications, medical sciences, etc. They range from a three week Diploma course in international law to a thirteen week course in leather technology to an 18 month MPhil course in women and development. NUFFIC (see above) publishes a booklet in English each year giving full details, including fees charged, and this is available from the Royal Netherlands Embassy in London.

Language courses
The Ministry of Education and Science runs summer courses in Dutch, for which scholarships are available for students of Dutch in this country. Apply to Ministry of Education and Science, Bureau Congresses, PO Box 25000, 2700 LZ Zoetermeer, tel (010 31 79) 53 19 11, and to the Embassy in London for details of scholarships.

Dutch courses are also organized throughout the year by Internationale Studieverblijven Organisatie Katwijk, De Zeeuw, Jan-Tooropstraat 4, 2225 XT Katwijk-aan-Zee. Tel (01718) 13533.

See also following publications:

— *Dutch language courses for foreign students,* NUFFIC (see above).
— *Non-university language courses* available from the Foreign Student Office, Oranje Nassaulaan 5, 1075 AH Amsterdam.
— *Study Holidays* (see p.174).

Other courses
Music courses for children and adults run by Vereniging voor Huismuziek, Utrechtsestraat 77, PO Box 350, 3400 AJ Ijsselstein, tel (010 31) 3408 05670.

Joint programmes
Contact The Ministry of Education and Science (see below).

Other useful addresses
Netherlands Board of Tourism, 25-28 Buckingham Gate, London SW1E 6LD. Tel (01) 630 0451.

Ministry of Education and Science, Directorate of International Relations, PO Box 25000, 2700 LZ Zoetermeer. Tel (010 31 20) 531911.

Student travel
NBBS, Rapenburg 8, Leiden.

HUNGARY

Language of tuition Hungarian.
Academic year September to June.
Best contacts for information
● Embassy of the Hungarian Peoples' Republic, 35 Eaton Place, London SW1. Tel (01) 235 7191/4048.

Postgraduate
Grants are available for study/research in any subject from the Hungarian Government through the British Council, tenable for five or ten months. Some prior knowledge of Hungarian desirable. You may also be able to fund postgraduate study and research in Hungary through:

The Royal Society, 6 Carlton House Terrace, London SW1Y 5AG.
The British Academy, 20 Cornwall Terrace, London NW1.
The Wellcome Trust, 1 Park Square West, London NW1.

Language courses
Courses in Hungarian are run in Budapest each year in July and August by International House Language School CHC, PO Box 95, Budapest 1364. Tel (010 361) 111 306. See also **Summer Schools** below.

Hungarian Government bursaries are available for people wishing to attend summer courses in Hungarian language and culture held each year at Debrecen. Apply through the British Council Specialist Tours Dept by February.

Special schemes
The Hungarian government offers scholarships to British undergraduates for study for one academic year at a Hungarian institution. This scheme is administered through the British Council, to whom application should be made.

Summer schools
A wide variety of summer courses are held at Hungarian universities each year. The subjects range from the Kodaly method of teaching music to Esperanto, to Hungarian language, folklore and history. Some of these courses are held in English. Details can be obtained by writing to The Society for the Dissemination of Science (Tudományos Ismeretterjesztö Társulat), Bródy Sándorutca 16, 1367 Budapest VIII.

Bursaries are also available for attendance at some of these summer schools. They cover fees and board and lodging, but not travel expenses. Apply through the British Council Specialist Tours Dept, 65 Davies Street, London W1Y 1AA.

Other useful addresses
Danube Travel, 6 Conduit Street, London W1R 9TG. Tel (01) 493 0263.

Student travel
EXPRESS, Szabadsag Ter 16, Budapest 1395.

ICELAND

Language of tuition Icelandic
Academic year September to June
Best contacts for information
- Ministry of Education, Hverfisgata 4-6, 150 Reykjavik.
- University of Iceland, Reykjavik.

Grants
The Icelandic government offers seven-month scholarships to British students (postgraduates or undergraduates who have completed at least two years of their degree course) with some knowledge of Icelandic, for study at the University of Iceland in the area of Icelandic studies. Contact the Icelandic Embassy, 1 Eaton Terrace, London SW1 8EY, tel (01) 730 5131, for further details and application forms, which should be submitted by end April each year.

Useful addresses
Iceland Tourist Information Bureau, 73 Grosvenor Street, London W1. Tel (01) 499 6721.

Student travel
IST, Studentaheimilinu, v/Hringbrant, 101 Reykjavik.

ITALY

Italy has 55 institutions of higher education, including 44 state universities and a further 9 private universities. As long as you fulfil the entrance requirements in theory you qualify for a place at a state university; in practice lack of room does limit admissions. Apart from degree courses, you can study **corsi singoli** for one year only (see Visiting Studentships below) and there is good provision for Italian as a foreign language course.

Best areas of study Art, Italian language, classical studies and general.

Language of tuition Italian.

Academic year November to May.

Best contacts for information

● Italian Cultural Institute, 39 Belgrave Square, London SW1X 8NX. Tel (01) 235 1461.

1st degree courses

Length

A full Italian university degree is known as a **laurea** and takes four or five years. The intermediate **diploma,** in certain subjects only, is a professional qualification which takes only two or three years to complete.

Contact

Full details of courses can be obtained from the institutions themselves: the Italian Cultural Institute can supply an address list. One is also contained in the Italian section of *Higher Education in the European Community* (see p.174). Application must be made in person at Italian Consulates by mid April:

Italian Consulate General, 38 Eaton Place, London SW1X 8AN.

Italian Consulate in Manchester, St James's Building, 79 Oxford Street, Mancheser M1 6FQ.

Italian Consulate General in Edinburgh, 2 Melville Crescent, Edinburgh EH3 7HW.

Entrance requirements

Two 'A' levels in relevant subjects, plus four good GCSEs in other subjects (ie different from the A level subjects). Candidates who do not have at least GCSE standard Italian must pass a preliminary language test before their applications can be processed. Entrance examinations proper are held at each university in September.

Cost/grants

Fees vary, but are likely to be in the region of £100-£200.

Maintenance grants are not generally available for first degrees.

Postgraduate
After the *laurea* it is possible to obtain two kinds of higher qualification at Italian universities: the **dottorato di recerca** (Doctorate) or a specialised **diploma** which is more of a professional qualification.

Contact
The universities directly for information. Applications must be made through the Consulates, as above.

Entrance requirements
A Master's degree is usually necessary, plus knowledge of Italian, as above.

Grants
The Italian government offers a number of scholarships and bursaries for postgraduate studies at Italian universities for periods of two and eight months. A Master's degree is normally required, together with good Italian. There are also Council of Europe Scholarships for studies and research lasting up to one academic year, and scholarships for study at the Scuola Normale Superore in Pisa. The Italian institute (see above) processes applications for all these and can supply further information. See also *Study Abroad* (p.174) for details of grants available for study in research in specific fields.

Visiting studentships
Students who have completed at least one year of a degree course elsewhere can apply to attend **corsi singoli** for a year at an Italian university. Under this scheme you are allowed to attend lectures in more than one faculty at the same time, and at the end you will get a certificate of attendance. If you pass the relevant exam, you will also get a certificate of achievement. Scholarships are available for this scheme. Further information and applications through the Italian Cultural Institute, as above.

Language Courses
There are two state institutions in Italy catering especially for foreigners wishing to learn Italian and open all year round. They are:

- Università per stranieri, Palazzo Gallanga, Piazza Fortebraccio, I-06100 Perugia. Tel (01039) 75 46344.

- Scuola di lingua e cultura italiana per stranieri, Via Banchi di Sotto 46, I-53100 Siena. Tel (01039) 577 49260.

The **Dante Alighieri Society** promotes Italian language and culture throughout the world, and runs classes all the year round at its centres in Rome, Florence, Milan and Venice. Write to Società Dante Alighieri:

Piazza Firenze 27, 00186 Rome. Tel (010 396) 687 3722.
Via Gino Capponi 4, 50121 Florence. Tel (010 3955) 247 8981.
Via Torriani 10, 20124 Milan. Tel (010 392) 669216.
Fondamenta Arsenale, Ponte de Purgatorio, 30122 Venice. Tel (01039 41) 528 9127.

The British Institute in Florence, Lungarno Guicciardini 9, 50125 Florence, tel (010 3955) 284031, runs one month courses in Italian language, drawing, history of art etc.

In addition there are summer courses run at various universities and a whole host of private institutions, including Inlingua, Eurocentres, and International House, whose UK offices (see p.29) can handle applications. Details of these and other privately run courses are contained in *Study Holidays* (see p.174) and in *Cultural and Language Courses in Italy* published by the Italian Cultural Institute in London. Courses may also be booked through:

- Cultural and Educational Services Abroad (see p.28).
- EuroAcademy (see p.28), Centro Turistico Studentesco, 33 Windmill Street, London W1P 1HH. Tel (01) 580 4554.
- School Journey Association, 48 Cavendish Road, London SW12 0DG. Tel (01) 675 6636.
- Oxford Tourists Service, Via Colpi 21, 38064 Folgaria (Tn). Tel (010 39 464) 71877.
- Pre-University Course in Italy, 18 Carlton Road, Oxford. Tel (0865) 56952.

Scholarships are available to students with A levels wishing to attend some of these courses: further details from the Italian Cultural Institute.

Other courses
The Italian Cultural Institute's booklet *Cultural and Language Courses in Italy* list courses in a whole range of subjects other than Italian language which are open to foreign students. These include art and craft of all kinds, fashion design, film, antiques, cookery,

archaeology, nuclear physics and data processing.

The International Centre for the Study of Mosaic, c/o Azienda Autonoma di Soggiorno e Turismo, Via S. Vitale 2, 48100 Ravenna, tel (010 39 544) 35755, runs international courses on mosaics at Lido Adriano.

Special schemes

The EEC runs a scheme whereby craftsmen and museum workers can be funded to attend courses in Venice on the conservation of cultural property: historic buildings, paintings and so on. Apply to the International Centre for the Study of the Preservation and Restoration of Cultural Property (ICCROM), Training Section, 13 via di San Michele, 00153 Rome, or to the European Centre for Training Craftsmen in the Conservation of the Architectural Heritage, Isola di San Servolo, Casella Postale 676, 30100 Venezia.

International university

The European University Institute in Florence was founded in 1971 to contribute to the 'development of the cultural and scientific heritage of Europe' through university teaching and research. It functions at postgraduate level only, offering one year Master's degrees or three years Doctoral degrees in history and cultural history, economics, law, and political and social science. Applications should be made by mid March each year to the address given, and candidates must also submit a detailed paper related to their research subject. Those accepted receive a grant amounting to £300-£400 per month, plus other expenses, from the DES (see below). There are presently about 150 students at the university, from all over the EC.

European University Institute, Academic Service, Badia Fiesolana, 5 via dei Roccettini, I-50016 San Domenico di Fiesole (Firenze). Tel (010 39 55) 477 931.

Dept of Education and Science, HFE IV Branch, Elizabeth House, York Road, London SE1 7HP.

Welfare

In each region there is an institute for *diritto allo studio*. It is responsible for student welfare, health and insurance, as well as organising sports and recreational activities for students in higher education.

Other useful addresses

Ministero degli Affari Esteri, Direzione Generale delle Relazioni Culturali con l'Estero, Piazza Farnesina 1, I-00100 Roma. Ministry

of Foreign affairs responsible for international cultural relations.
Ministero della Pubblica Istruzione, Viale Trastevere 76-Am, 00153
Rome.
Dante Alighieri Society, St Patrick's International Centre, 24 Great
Chapel Street, London W1V 3AF. Tel (01) 385 2800. Also at 15
Kensington High Street, London W8 5NP. Tel (01) 376 1148.
Italian State Tourist Office, 1 Prince's Street, London W1R 8AY.
Tel (01) 408 1254.
Association of Teachers of Italian, 14 Lilyville Road, London SW6
5DW. Tel (01) 736 3710.

Student travel
CTS, Via Nazionale 66, Rome.

LUXEMBOURG

Luxembourg is unique among the developed nations in that it does
not have a higher education system. The only opportunities that exist
are given below.

Language of tuition Normally French.
Academic year October to July.
Best contacts for information
● Orientation Scolaire et Services Sociaux du Ministère de l'Educa-
  tion Nationale, 7 rue Pierre d'Aspelt, L-1142 Luxembourg. Tel
  (010 352) 4794 555.

First year university courses
These are held at the Centre Universitaire de Luxembourg. There
is a limited range of subjects for students intending to continue their
studies at French or Belgian universities.

Contact
Centre Universitaire, Cours Universitaires, Département des
Sciences, Place Auguste-Laurent, L-1921 Luxembourg (for Sciences);
and Centre Universitaire, Cours Universitaires, 162a Avenue de la
Faïencerie, L-1511 Luxembourg (for other subjects).

Entrance requirements
Full secondary education and good enough French to follow the
course.

Cost
There are no tuition fees, but no grants for foreign students either.
The Departement de Droit et des Sciences Economiques also runs two
year courses in data processing, commerce and banking, and business
administration.

Postgraduate
Institut Universitaire International, 162a avenue de la Faïencerie,
L-1511 Luxembourg: three or four week courses in comparative law,
European studies or political economy. Applicants must have a
university degree or professional qualification in one of these areas.
Some bursaries may be available.

Institut Européen pour la Gestion de l'Information, 13 rue de
Bragance, L-1255 Luxembourg: training in data management for
graduates in data processing or similar fields.

Other courses
Institut Supérieur de Technologie, rue Richard Coudenhove-Kalergi,
L-1359 Luxembourg. Three year diploma courses in engineering
(various branches) and computer science.

Summer courses
These are organised by the following:
Cercle Européen pour la Propagation des Arts, 19 rue de l'Ecole,
L-6235 Beidweiler. For students of Art some bursaries may be
available.

International Courses for Music Performance, Conservatoire de
Musique, 33 rue Charles Martel, L-2134, Luxembourg. For advanced
music students.

Other useful addresses
Luxembourg Embassy, 27 Wilton Crescent, London SW1. Tel (01)
235 6961.
Ministère de l'Education Nationale, 6 boulevard Royal, 2449
Luxembourg. Tel (010 352) 47941.

NORWAY

Language of tuition Norwegian.
Academic year September to June, divided into two semesters.
Best contacts for information

● In the first instance, the Royal Norwegian Embassy, 25 Belgrave Square, London SW1X 8QD. Tel (01) 235 7151.

1st degree courses

Length Four or five years.

Contact
The universities themselves — there are just four plus various specialised colleges. Addresses from the Norwegian Embassy.

Entrance requirements
Minimum of two 'A' levels, or equivalent, plus knowledge of Norwegian; see Language Courses below.

Cost/grants
Tuition is free. Under certain circumstances loans may be offered to foreign students for help with living expenses.

Postgraduate

Contact The university concerned, as above.

Entrance requirements At least a Bachelor's degree, in some cases a Master's.

Grants
Nine month scholarships are offered to British graduates by the Norwegian government. Apply to the Norwegian Embassy by 31st December each year.

Twelve-month post-doctoral research grants are available for applied research in science or engineering. Apply to: Royal Norwegian Council for Scientific and Industrial Research, Sognsveien 72, 0855 Oslo 8, by 1st December each year.

Nine-month Council of Europe scholarships are available for graduates in any subject. Apply to Norwegian Ministry of Foreign Affairs, Press and Cultural Relations Dept, Scholarships Section, PO Box 8114, Dep, 0032 Oslo 1, by 1st April each year.

Language Courses
One year Norwegian language courses — normally compulsory for intending students at Norwegian universities — are held at the

University of Oslo. For full information write to University of Oslo, Office for Foreign Students, PO Box 1081, Blindern, Oslo 3.

Six week summer courses are held at the University of Oslo in Norwegian language and culture. Contact address as above.

Three week intensive summer courses are run by the University of Bergen. Some scholarships may be available. Apply to The Nordic Institute, University of Bergen, Sydenes plass 9, 5000 Bergen.

International summer school

The University of Oslo runs an International Summer School. This includes, in English, general courses on Norway and Norwegian language, plus postgraduate courses in subjects such as education, urban planning, and health services. Scholarships are available for those wishing to attend. Full details of each year's programme can be obtained from International Summer School, University of Oslo, PO Box 10, Blindern, 0313 Oslo 3.

Special schemes

Grants are available for young workers and students who wish to study at Norwegian Folk High Schools. Apply to the Norwegian Embassy by 14th March each year.

Other useful addresses

Norwegian Ministry of Foreign Affairs, Press and Cultural Relations Dept, PO Box 8114, Oslo 1 (information service for foreign students).

Norwegian National Tourist Office, 20 Pall Mall, London SW1Y 5NE. Tel (01) 839 6255.

Anglo-Norse Society, 25 Belgrave Square, London SW1. Tel (01) 235 7151.

Student travel
UR, Universitetssentret, Blindern, PO Box 55, Oslo 3.

POLAND

Best areas of study sociology, mathematics, geography and geology, Polish and Polish studies.
Language of tuition Polish.
Academic year October to June.
Best contacts for information
● Polish Cultural Institute, 34 Portland Place, London W1N 3DG.

Tel (01) 636 6032-3.

Postgraduate

Sixteen scholarships are available annually for British postgraduates, covering tuition, board and lodging for ten months or less, plus travel expenses from the British Council. Applicants wishing to specialise in Polish studies must speak Polish or another Slavonic language. Apply by 31st December to the British Council, 65 Davies Street, London W1Y 2AA. A special Chopin Fellowship is awarded to a musician each year under the same conditions.

There are also short-term bursaries available (three months or less) for postgraduate or post-doctoral research to be carried out in Poland. Again, apply through the British Council.

Language courses

One year courses are held at the university of Lódz and the Marie Sklodowska-Curie University at Lublin; there are also summer courses in Polish language, literature and culture at the University of Warsaw, 00927 Warsaw 64. Further details from the Polish Institute.

The relevant section of the Central Bureau's publication *Study Holidays* contains details of a number of courses at Polish universities, which may be booked through the Polish Consulate General, 73 New Cavendish Street, London W1N 7RB. Tel (01) 636 4533.

Other useful addresses

Ministry of Science, Higher Education and Technology, 6-8 Miodowa Street, 00251 Warszawa.

Polorbis Travel Ltd, 82 Mortimer Street, London W1N 7DE. Tel (01) 637 4971.

Student travel
Almatur, Ordynacka Street 9, Warsaw 00953.

PORTUGAL

Portugal has only four traditional universities, two in Lisbon, the others in Porto and Coimbra. Since 1973 it has been expanding its higher education system to include new universities and university institutes in other regions. The *Instituto de Cultura e Língua Portuguesa* promotes Portuguese for foreigners courses strongly, even offering some scholarships (see below).

Language of tuition Portuguese.

Academic year October to July.

Best contacts for information

● Portuguese Embassy, Cultural Section, 11 Belgrave Square, London SW1X 8PP. Tel (01) 235 5331.

● Ministério da Educacao e Cultura, Av 5 de Outubro 107, 1000 Lisboa.

1st degree courses

Length

Four to six years for a **licenciatura** degree. Other technical degrees **(bacharelato)** and diplomas may be completed in three years.

Contact

The universities themselves. A list may be obtained from either of the addresses given above, or see *Time Off in Spain and Portugal* (Horizon Books) or *Higher Education in the European Community* (see p.174). Both of these publications provide detailed background information.

Entrance requirements

'A' levels, an entrance exam, and good knowledge of Portuguese.

Cost

Fees are minimal, but no grants are normally available for maintenance costs.

Postgraduate

The Portuguese Master's degree is known as the **mestrado;** a doctorate as a **doutoramento.**

Contact The universities directly, see above.

Entrance requirements

The equivalent of the **licenciatura:** normally a Master's degree.

Grants

For study or research in the area of Portuguese language and culture:

● Instituto de Cultura e Língua Portuguese, Praca do Príncipe Real 14-1⁰, 1200 Lisboa, tels (01) 364508 and (01) 363885.

● Calouste Gulbenkian Foundation, International Dept, Av de

Berna 45a, 1093 Lisboa.

In other areas:

● The Instituto Nacional de Investigacao Científica offers grants for teacher-training in Portugal for up to three years if you can get a sponsoring institution outside Portugal to guarantee you a job as a teacher of Portuguese afterwards.

● The Instituto Nacional de Investigacao Científica offers grants for one academic year to postgraduates or students in their final year for study in any subject. Some knowledge of Portuguese is necessary. Apply through the Portuguese Embassy (see above) by 31st March.

Language Courses

Summer courses in Portuguese language and culture are held at the following universities:

University of Lisbon, Departamento de Língua e Cultura Portuguesa, Faculdade de Letras de Lisboa, Cidade Universitária, 1699 Lisboa.

New University of Lisbon, Departamento de Estudos Anglo-Portugueses, Faculdade de Ciencias Sociais e Humanas, Av de Berna 24, 1000 Lisboa.

Universidade de Coimbra, Faculdade de Letras, Gabinete de Relacaoes Internacionais, 3049 Coimbra.

Universidade de Aveiro, Faculdade de Letras, R. Dr. Mario Sacramente 62, Aveiro.

The Universities of Lisbon and Coimbra also offer courses lasting a full academic year. Grants are available covering the cost of tuition fees for all these courses. Apply to Instituto de Cultura et Lingua Portuguesa, as above.

There are also private language schools open throughout the year, for example:

Centro Audio Visual de Linguas, Praca Luis de Camoes 36-3⁰, Lisboa. Tel (010 3511) 364988.

Centro de Linguas, Av dea República 14, Lisboa. Tel (010 3511) 533733.

Inlingua, Rua Goncalo Cristovao 217, 4000 Porto. Tel (010 3512) 319313.

For a full list, apply to the Portuguese Embassy, or see *Time Off in Spain and Portugal* (p.174) or *Study Holidays* (p.174).

British agencies which can arrange Portuguese courses for you in Portugal include

Euroyouth
International House
Inlingua
Cultural and Educational Services Abroad
EuroAcademy

See p.28-29 for addresses.

Other useful addresses
Portuguese National Tourist Office, New Bond House, New Bond Street, London W1Y 0NP. Tel (01) 493 3873.

Hispanic and Luso-Brazilian Council, Canning House, 2 Belgrave Square, London SW1X 8PJ. Tel (01) 235 2303.

Student travel
TAGUS, Rua Camillo Castelo Branco 20, 1100 Lisbon.

ROMANIA

Language of tuition Romanian.
Academic year September to July.
Best contacts for information
● Ministry of Education, Foreign Students Dept, Str. Spiru Haret nr. 12, 70738 Bucharest.
● Embassy of the Socialist Republic of Romania, 4 Palace Green, London W8 4QD. Tel (01) 937 9666-9.

Language courses
The Romanian government offers bursaries to British people wanting to attend summer schools in Romanian language and culture, held in Bucharest and in Cluj each year. Fees, board and lodging are included but not travel expenses. Apply through the British Council Specialist Tours Dept (see p.75).

Useful addresses
National Tourist Office of Romania, 98-99 Jermyn Street, London SW1Y 6EF. Tel (01) 930 8812.

Student travel
BTTR, 4/6 Onesti Street, Bucharest.

SPAIN

Spain has 30 full universities and many more university level institutions, and literally hundreds of Spanish for Foreigners courses.

Language of tuition Spanish.
Academic year October to May.
Best contacts for information
- Spanish Embassy Education Office, 20 Peel Street, London W8 7PD. Tel (01) 727 2462.
- *Time Off in Spain and Portugal* (Tinsley, Horizon Books, 1989).

1st degree courses

Length
A full degree or *licenciatura* takes five years. A university Diploma can be completed in three, as can courses leading to qualifications in areas such as teaching, nursing, tourism, business studies, and so on.

Contact
The universities themselves. A list of those offering the subject you are interested in can be obtained from the Spanish Embassy Education Office, or see latest edition of *Higher Education in the European Community*.

Entrance requirements
Minimum of five GCSE' and two 'A' levels, plus an entrance exam which can be taken in this country. For details contact Centro de Apoyo de la UNED, 317 Portobello Road, London W10. Tel (01) 986 8718 (after 4pm). For the exam you must offer three subjects (chosen from specified groups) as well as Spanish language, so in effect you need to have studied three A levels.

Cost
Tuitional fees are minimal, but no grants are available for maintenance costs.

Postgraduate

Contact
The Faculty of the university where you wish to study. See above.

Entrance requirements
Normally you would already need to have a Master's degree, as there is no degree in Spain between the five year **licenciatura** and the **doctorado**. Some private institutions offer Master's degrees, notably the bilingual (English-Spanish) MBA programme run by the University of Navarre in Barcelona, Instituto de Estudios Superiores de la Empresa, Avda Pearson 21, 08034 Barcelona. Tel (010 343) 204 4000.

Grants
These are offered by the Consejo Superior de Investigaciones Científicas and the Ministerio de Asuntos Exteriores to British graduates with some knowledge of Spanish. Apply in both instances to the Spanish Embassy, Minister for Cultural Affairs, 24 Belgrave Square, London SW1. Phone for details: (01) 235 2484/5. For details of other grants which may be available, contact the Subdirección General de Becas y Ayudas al Estudio, Torrelaguna 58, 28027 Madrid. Tel (010 341) 408 2008.

Language Courses

The most comprehensive list of Spanish language courses is contained in *Time Off in Spain and Portugal* (see above). Universities like Madrid and Salamanca offer courses lasting a term or an academic year, and also summer courses:

Secretaría de los Cursos para Extranjeros, Facultad de Filosofía y Letras, Universidad Complutense, Ciudad Universitaria, 28040 Madrid. Tel (010 341) 243 3448.

Universidad de Salamanca, Secretaría de la Facultad de Filología, Plaza de Anaya, Salamanca.

There are also many private language schools, large and small, up and down the country. These include (see p.29):

Inlingua
International House
Eurocentres
or book through (see p.28):
Cultural and Educational Services Abroad
Euro-Academy Ltd
John Galleymore

Spain's other languages

There are also courses in Spain's other languages, Catalan, Basque (Euskera) and Galician:

— *Catalan* Escola Oficial d'Idiomes, Avda Drassanes, 08001 Barcelona. Tel (010 343) 29 34 12.

— *Euskera* Euskalduntze Alfabetantze Koordinakundea, Diputazio Kalea 3, 48009 Bilbao. Tel (010 344) 423 15 52.

— *Galician* Secretaría de Cursos de Galego, Instituto da Lingua Galega, Praza da Universidade 4, 15703 Santiago de Compostela. Tel (010 3481) 56 52 83.

International University

The Universidad Internacional Menéndez Pelayo runs (during the summer months only) in a former royal palace in Santander, on the north coast of Spain. Its programme embraces language and culture courses for foreigners, lectures on topical themes by well-known speakers, theatre workshops, music classes, film shows and concerts, and a range of other peripheral events. For details all the year round, contact: UIMP, Amador de los Rios 1, 28010 Madrid. Tel (010 341) 410 4901.

Joint programmes

ERASMUS programmes.

Other useful addresses

Spanish National Tourist Office, 57-58 St James Street, London SW1. Tel (01) 499 0101.

Spanish Institute, 102 Eaton Square, London SW1. Tel (01) 235 1481/5.

Spanish Consulate, 20 Draycott Place, London SW3. Tel (01) 581 5921-6.

Hispanic and Luso-Brazilian Council, Canning House, 2 Belgrave Square, London SW1. Tel (01) 235 2303.

Ministerio de Educación y Ciencia, Alcalá 34, 28014 Madrid. Tel (010 341) 232 1300.

Student travel
TIVE, Fernando el Católico 88, 28015 Madrid. Tel (010 341) 449 6800, and provincial branches.

SWEDEN

There are good well organised opportunities for the foreign student who can get funding.

Language of tuition Swedish, with some English at postgraduate level; see below.

Academic year End August to beginning June, divided into two terms.

Best contacts for information
- Swedish Embassy, 11 Montagu Place, London W1H 2AL. Tel (01) 724 2101.
- Swedish Institute, PO Box 7434, S-103 91 Stockholm, Sweden.

1st degree courses

Length
2-5½ years. The length of courses is expressed in terms of 'points'. One point is equal to one week of full time study. Higher education is unified and includes professional-type studies not encompassed by the university system in other countries.

Contact
The Swedish Embassy, which handles applications for first degree courses. The Embassy can supply a most useful and well-produced document entitled *Studying in Sweden: Higher Education for Visiting Students,* giving details of many courses and how to apply. It suggests however writing direct to the university of your choice (a list is included) to obtain further information before making an application.

Entrance requirements
11 years of schooling from age 6, knowledge of Swedish (see **Language Courses** below), knowledge of English, and a residence permit. You apply for the latter at the same time as you apply for a university place, through the Embassy. Extra entrance requirements are often imposed for subjects where there is heavy competition for places.

Cost/grants
Tuition is free, although there is a small compulsory contribution payable to the Students Union. Living expenses are high however, calculated at 3,800 Krona per month (= £380 — 1987/88 figures). British students taking first degrees in Sweden aren't normally eligible for grants, and will need to show that they can supply this figure out of their own funds.

Postgraduate

Contact
See the *Studying in Sweden* handbook, as above. Applications have
to be made to the university department concerned, not to the
Embassy.

Entrance requirements
A first degree — for some studies a Master's too — and a good
knowledge of English. Knowledge of Swedish is not always necessary;
check with the university department concerned.

Grants
A number of postgraduate scholarships are open to British students;
they are generally restricted to specialist or scientific areas where
study in Sweden can offer special advantages. Applications should
be received by the Swedish Institute in Stockholm (see above) by 1st
December each year.

The Swedish Government offers four postgraduate scholarships
each year for study and research to members of British universities
and colleges, lasting four or eight months. Applications for these
are handled by the British Council, OEAD, 65 Davies Street, London
W1Y 2AA.

Other 'Guest Scholarships' are offered by the Swedish Institute,
address as above.

Language courses
The **Preparatory Swedish Language Course** is a one-year course, held
at various universities in Sweden, designed to give foreign students
a good enough knowledge of Swedish to enable them to take a degree
at a Swedish university. 300 places are available each year. Applications are handled by the Swedish Embassy at the same time as applications for first degree courses.

Swedish language summer schools: courses last between two and
ten weeks and are run by a number of organisations including:

- International Swedish University Programs, Skomakaregatan 8,
  S-223 50 Lund. Tel **(010 46) 46 151 784.**
- Kursverksamheten Vid Stockholms Universitet, Box 7845, S-103
  98 Stockholm. Tel **(010 468) 789 4100.**
- Uppsala University International Summer Session, Box 256,
  S-751 05 Uppsala. Tel **(010 4618) 155 400.**

Details of dates, fees etc are contained in a booklet entitled *Svenska Institutets Internationalla Sommarkurser,* available from the Swedish Embassy from January or February each year, or write direct to the addresses given above.

Joint programmes/special schemes
A number of postgraduate programmes are being developed in English for an international market, as follows:

● One year Diploma Course in Social Sciences and Law, offered by: Institute for English Speaking Students, Stockholm University, S-106 91 Stockholm.

● International Master's Degrees in various subject areas, through the Swedish International University Consortium, c/o UHA, Box 45501, S-140 30 Stockholm.

For those who understand Swedish there is a wide range of summer schools and courses organised by the Swedish Institute; details are contained in the aforementioned guide *Internationella Sommarkurser,* available direct from the Swedish Institute in Stockholm, or from the Swedish Embassy.

Folk high schools
These were founded in Sweden and other Scandinavian countries in the mid nineteenth century to give rural adults a better general education. They are run by voluntary organisations, with no official syllabus, but a high degree of student participation in their running. They can prepare students for university entrance. Further details from the Swedish Institute in Stockholm, see above.

Welfare
The Students Unions (membership compulsory) run specialist welfare services (student health service, housing foundations etc) which are available to students in addition to the normal services. Only a minority of students live in university accommodation, as it is policy to integrate students into general housing, not special student accommodation. For further information on all aspects of welfare contact: National Association of Student Unions in Sweden (SFS), St Eriksplan 2, S-113 20 Stockholm.

Other useful addresses
The National Board of Universities and Colleges (UHÄ), Box 45501, S-14030 Stockholm: Central Government agency which supervises

the Higher Education system.

Swedish National Tourist Office, 3 Cork Street, London W1X 1HA. Tel (01) 437 5816.

Student travel
SFS-Resor, Drottninggatan 89, S-10430 Stockholm.
International Youth Centre, Valhallavagen 142, S-11524 Stockholm.

SWITZERLAND

The Swiss education system is characterised by its extreme variety and diversity, with responsibility for education being carried by each of the 26 different cantons. It enjoys a good reputation worldwide, and the private sector in particular has always attracted large numbers of foreign students.

Language of tuition German, French and others.
Academic year October to July, divided into two semesters.
Best contacts for information
● In the first instance, the Swiss Embassy in London, 16-18 Montagu Place, London W1H 2BQ. Tel (01) 723 0701.

1st degree courses

Length Three or four years minimum, depending on institution.

Contact
The Secretariat of the University concerned. Addresses, together with useful general information, are contained in a booklet published by the Swiss National Tourist Office entitled *The Swiss Universities,* available from the Swiss Embassy in London (see above). Information on syllabuses at the different universities may also be obtained from the Central Office of the Swiss Universities, Sophienstrasse 2, CH-8032 Zurich. Tel (010 411) 47 02 32.

Entrance requirements
'A' levels, or other equivalent to the Swiss matriculation certificate. You must also have an adequate knowledge, which may be examined, of the language of instruction (French at Geneva, Lausanne, Neuchâtel and Fribourg Universities, German at the rest). Candidates without these entrance requirements may prepare and sit an entrance examination held twice yearly in Fribourg; information from the

Secretariat of the University Preparatory Courses, Route du Jura 1, CH-1700 Fribourg, tel (010 41) 37 26 41 23. Universities retain the right of admission, and limit the number of foreign students they accept in certain fields, especially medicine.

Cost/grants
Tuition fees are comparatively low: between SFr 350 and 800 pa. However Swiss living expenses are considerable. No scholarships are available for undergraduate studies.

Postgraduate

Contact As for first degrees, see above.

Entrance requirements
Graduate status (under 35) and knowledge of the language, as above.

Grants
Swiss government scholarships of nine months duration: usually two each year for study in any field, plus several more specifically for music or art. Applications through the Swiss Embassy, by mid December each year.

Council of Europe Scholarships, nine months, any field: apply to the Commission Fédérale des Bourses pour Étudiants Étrangers, Route du Jura 1, CH-1700 Fribourg, by mid January.

One scholarship is available each year for a British student with knowledge of French for postgraduate study at the University of Neuchâtel. Apply to the Université de Neuchâtel, Bourses pour Étudiants Britanniques, Secrétariat Général, CH-2000 Neuchâtel, by mid March.

Visiting studentships
Students who do not meet entrance requirements or do not wish to enrol on a full course may attend lectures as guest students. Apply direct to the universities concerned.

Language courses
French language and culture courses are held each summer at the universities of Geneva, Lausanne and Neuchâtel. Information about these may be obtained from the Swiss National Tourist Office, Swiss Centre, 1 New Coventry Street, London W1V 3HG. Tel (01) 734 1291. Or you can apply direct to:

- Université de Lausanne, Secrétariat des Cours de Vacances, BFSH 2 Dorigny, CH-1015, tel (010 4121) 46 45 19.
- Université de Neuchâtel, Faculté des Lettres, Cours de Vacances, 26 Avenue du Premier Mars, CH-2000 Neuchâtel, tel (010 4138) 25 38 51.

Both Inlingua and Eurocentres have branches in Switzerland offering French as a foreign language. Apply through their UK offices, addresses on p.29. You can also book French language courses through Cultural and Educational Services Abroad, see p.28. The American School in Switzerland, 6926 Montagnola-Lugano, tel (010 4193) 54 64 71 offers summer language programmes in both French and Italian, for ages 12-18 only.

For courses in German, apply to: Ferienkurs der Stadt Winterthur, Baceggliweg 22, CH-8405 Winterthur; and International Teen Camp, PO Box 122, CH-1012 Chailly-s-Lausanne, tel (010 4121) 22 67 78 and (010 4121) 32 11 22.

For addresses of other institutions offering courses in French and Italian, see *Study Holidays*.

Summer schools
International music summer schools for young people are organised by:
- Jeunesses Musicales de Suisse, Maison de la Radio, Case postale 233, CH-1211 Geneva, tel (010 4122) 28 70 64.
- Kinder-Musik-Institut Alex und Christine Eckert, Aeschenplatz 2, CH-4051 Basle, tel (010 4161) 701136.

Private schools
There are a large number of private schools and academies in Switzerland keen to attract foreign students for a wide range of studies; they offer everything from primary and secondary education, to 'finishing schools', courses in languages, management, secretarial studies, etc. A booklet providing information on these, entitled *Private Schools in Switzerland* is available from the Swiss Embassy, or through the Swiss Federation of Private Schools, 40 rue des Vollandes, CH-1211 Genève 6, tel (010 4122) 35 57 06 (French-speaking sector); or Postfach 265, CH-3097 Liebefeld-Bern, tel (010 4191) 59 65 55 (German-speaking sector). For help in choosing a private school in Switzerland, contact Gabbitas Truman and Thring, 6-8 Sackville Street, Piccadilly, London W1X 2BR, tel (01) 734 0161.

Other useful addresses
Verband Schweizerischer Studentenschaften (Swiss Student Societies
Organisation), Erlachstrasse 9, CH-3012 Berne.
Swiss National Tourist Office, Swiss Centre, 1 New Coventry
Street, London W1V 8EE, tel (01) 734 1921.

Student travel
SSR, Bäckerstrasse 52, CH-8026 Zurich.

TURKEY

Language of tuition Generally Turkish, but English is used at the
Technical University of the Middle East, Inönö Caddesi, Ankara,
and at certain faculties of other institutions.
Academic year October to June.
Best contacts for information
- Turkish Embassy, Education Counsellor, Camelot House, 76
Brompton Road, London SW3. Tel (01) 584 4062.
- Ministry of Education, Ankara.

Postgraduate grants
Several eight-month scholarships for research at institutions in
Turkey are offered each year to British graduates. Apply in March
each year to the Turkish Embassy Education counsellor, as above.

Language courses
Summer courses in Turkish language (including beginners) are held
at:
Ankara University, Turkish Language Centre, Dil ve Tarih-
Cografya Fakultesi, Sihhiye, Ankara. Tel (010 9041) 10 32 80/384;
and at Istanbul University, Turk Dili ve Kulturu yaz Kurlari Burosu,
Istanbul. Tel (010 901) 520 1365 and 528 6904.
About eight scholarships are available each year for attending the
course at Istanbul University. Apply in March to the Education
Counsellor, as above.

Useful addresses
Turkish Embassy (general enquiries), 43 Belgrave Square, London
SW1X 8PA. Tel (01) 235 5252.
Turkish Tourist Office, 1st Floor, 170-173 Piccadilly, London
W1V 9DD. Tel (01) 734 8681.

Student travel
GENCTUR, Yerebatan Cad 15/3, Sultanahmet, Istanbul.
7-Tur, Abdülhakhamid Cad 2/3, Taksim, Istanbul.

USSR

The USSR has a vast education system; however, possibilities for British students are restricted to the schemes detailed below:

Language of tuition Russian, and some English.
Academic year September to July.
Best contacts for information
● British Embassy Cultural Section, Naberezhanaya Morisa, Toreza 14, Moscow 109072. Tel (010 7095) 233 4507.

Postgraduate
A large number of scholarships are available for two/three month, five month or ten month periods of study/research in the USSR. They are open to graduates in any field, although a working knowledge of Russian is usually necessary. Scholarships cover tuition, board and lodging, and the British Council pays the fares. Apply through the British Council, 65 Davies Street, London W1Y 2AA, by October each year.

Language courses
If you want to study Russian *in situ,* the following schemes are available:

1. A one-month course in Leningrad for teachers or intending teachers of Russian, subsidised by Soviet authorities and the British Council. Apply by mid March to the Specialist Tours Dept.

2. Year Abroad schemes for undergraduate students of Russian. Students normally attend a course of study either at the University of Vornezh or the Maurice Thorenz Institute in Moscow. Travel is normally covered by the LEA grant. Apply, through the Department of Russian at your own institution, to the Russian Language Undergraduate Study Committee, by mid November each year.

3. Three-month schemes for undergraduate students of Russian. As above, but for a shorter period and at different Russian

universities.

4. One-month language and education visits for student teachers or Russian specialists interested in education. Apply through your own college department by November.

5. Various schemes are organised by the Society for Cultural Relations with the USSR, 320 Brixton Road, London SW9 6AB, tel (01) 274 2282. These include a seminar for teachers of Russian five or ten month studentships at the Pushkin Institute, Moscow, Russian language courses, exchanges, visits and so on.

Other useful addresses
Embassy of the USSR, 13 Kensington Palace Gardens, London W8 4QX. Tel (01) 229 3628.

Intourist Moscow Ltd, 292 Regent Street, London W1. Tel (01) 631 1252.

Progressive Tours, 12 Porchester Place, London W2 2BS. Tel (01) 262 1676.

Student travel
SPUTNIK, 15 Vorobyovskoye Chaussée 117946, Moscow V334.

YUGOSLAVIA

Language of tuition Serbo-Croat, Slovenian, Macedonian.
Academic year September to June.
Best contacts for information
● Federal Institute for International Co-operation in Education, Culture and Technology, Kosancicev venac 29, 11000 Belgrade.
● Embassy of the Socialist Federal Republic of Yugoslavia, 5 Lexham Gardens, London W8 5JJ. Tel (01) 370 6105-9.

Postgraduate
Scholarships for study in Yugoslavia for periods of three months to a year (or more) are offered to British graduates who preferably have some basic knowledge of one of the Yugoslavian languages, under a scheme administered by the British Council, which can provide further information and application forms.

Language courses
Two week courses in Slovenian language and literature are open to

sfudent Slavists as well as established teachers and researchers; they
are held each year at the University of Ljublijana. Apply to Faculty
of Philosophy, University of Ljublijana, Askerceva 12, 61000
Ljublijana.

Bursaries are available for British Slavists wishing to attend this
and other summer schools in Slovenian or Macedonian studies. Apply through the British Council Specialist Tours Dept, by February.

For courses in Serbo-Croat, see the relevant section of *Study
Holidays,* published by the Central Bureau.

Special schemes

A wide variety of short courses, seminars and conferences — often
held in English — are organised throughout the year by the Inter-
University Centre, Frana Bulica 4, 50000 Dubrovnik. Apply directly for details.

Other useful addresses

Yugoslav National Tourist Office, 143-147 Regent Street, London
W1R 8AE. Tel (01) 734 5243.

Student travel
YUS, Knez Milhailova 50, 11000 Belgrade.

The Rest of the World

This section includes countries in:

- Latin America
- Arab world
- Asia
- Africa

It groups together many 'long haul' destinations for study abroad, and covers an immense range of countries, from the rich and developed like Japan, to some of the poorest where very little educational provision exists at any level, to areas of the world where war or political instability rules out practically any opportunity for study.

LATIN AND CENTRAL AMERICA

The traffic in students between Latin America and the UK has traditionally been in the reverse direction from that dealt with in this book. Education in many Latin American states has suffered from poor funding, lack of academic freedom and the disruption of its activities through strikes or military or official shutdowns. The situation today in many countries is a classically top-heavy education system. At the bottom, basic literacy is an objective still far from being achieved, while at the top higher education is fairly well developed. In many countries the influence of the Napoleonic system — designed primarily to regulate professional qualifications — is very much in evidence. Foreigners can usually gain access to studies provided they pay their own way, but there may be considerable bureaucratic difficulties to be overcome in getting British qualifications recognised and in obtaining the necessary visas and paperwork. Bear in mind that if the system is designed for doling out professional certificates rather than to provide 'education' as we understand it, the experience may be of limited value.

A number of countries offer established schemes for foreign

students; although these tend to be aimed at the US market, British students can also take advantage of them. A case in point is the **Caribbean Campus Program** run by the InterAmerican Institute of Puerto Rico in Guadeloupe, Martinique, the Dominican Republic, Haiti and Jamaica. For further details apply to the Director at Penthouse G, Condominium El Monte North, Hato Rey, Puerto Rico 00918, USA.

There are also opportunities from the 'development' angle. In fact the sheer size and scope of the continent offers a wealth of possibilities for both study and research. The best countries are Mexico (for Spanish speakers) and Brazil (if you speak Portuguese).

Useful addresses

- Asociación Panamericana de Instituciones de Crédito Educativo (APICE), calle 38 no. 8.56, Apartado aereo 17388, Bogotá, Colombia. This organisation acts as an information clearing house for higher education throughout the region; it produces a useful publication entitled *Estudios Universitarios y de Postgrado en America Latina y el Caribe.*

- Association of Caribbean University and Research Institutes, PO Box 11532, Caparra Heights Station, San Juan, Puerto Rico 00922.

- Organización de Universidades de América Latina, Pontificia Universidad Católica Argentina 'Santa María de los Buenos Aires', Juncal 1912, Buenos Aires, Argentina. Co-ordinates the Catholic universities of Latin America.

- Unión de Universidades de América Latina, Centro de Información y Documentatión Universitaria, Apartado Postal 70232, Edificio UDUAL, Ciudad Universitaria, Delegación de Coyoacán, 04510-Mexico DF.

- Hispanic and Luso-Brazilian Council, Canning House, 2 Belgrave Square, London SW1X 8PJ. Tel (01) 235 2303. A good source of information on educational opportunities in Latin America, Spain and Portugal.

ARAB COUNTRIES

The richness of Arab history and culture should provide good study possibilities for historians, archaeologists, Arabists and social scientists of all kinds. However actual opportunities are severely limited, and in some cases completely eliminated, by one or more of the following in most Arab states:

- political instability
- lack of opportunities for women
- lack of cultural exchange agreements

The countries which offer the best possibilities are Egypt, Tunisia and Morocco.

Useful addresses

Arab League Educational, Scientific and Cultural Organisation (ALESCO), Khartoum International Institute for Arabic Language, PO Box 26, Eastern Diems, Khartoum, Sudan.

Other Arab States

The study possibilities in the various other Arab states are scant, but contact addresses are included here for the sake of completeness:

Embassy of the Sultanate of Oman, 44a-44b Montpelier Avenue, London SW7 1JJ. Tel (01) 584 6782.

Embassy of the State of Qatar, 27 Chesham Place, London SW1X 8HG. Tel (01) 235 0851.

Embassy of the United Arab Emirates, 30 Prince's Gate, London SW7 1PT. Tel (01) 581 1281.

Embassy of the People's Democratic Republic of Yemen, 57 Cromwell Road, London SW7 2ED. Tel (01) 584 6607.

Embassy of the Yemen Arab Republic, 41 South Street, London W1Y 5PD. Tel (01) 629 9905-8.

THE FAR EAST

An area of the world with immense potential for study and research, and one that has perhaps been underexploited by British scholars.

AFRICA

The opportunities for 'study' in many of the countries listed in this chapter would perhaps better be considered as opportunities for taking part in aid and development work.

AFGHANISTAN

Language of tuition Pashto and Dari (Persian).
Academic year March to January.
Best contacts for information
● Vice Chancellor, Kabul University, Kabul.
● Embassy of the Democratic Republic of Afghanistan, 31 Prince's Gate, London SW7 1QQ. Tel (01) 589 8891.

Language courses
Available as one year preparatory courses for foreign students proposing to study at Kabul University.

ALGERIA

Language of tuition Arabic or French.
Academic year October to July.
Best contacts for information
● Algerian Embassy, 54 Holland Park, London W11 3RS. Tel (01) 221 7800.

1st degree and postgraduate courses
Open to foreign students fulfilling the necessary entrance requirements — contact the university concerned. There are universities in Algiers, Annaba, Constantine and Oran, as well as other university-type institutions in other towns. See Embassy for addresses.

ARGENTINA

Argentina offers a good range of study opportunities, although these are mostly aimed at Latin American and US citizens; the UK has few established links with Argentinian institutions and only now are contacts being restored following the Falklands war. There are universities in all the main towns and cities: Cordoba, Buenos Aires (several institutions), Paraná, La Plata, Santa Fé, Resistencia, Rosario, Bahía Blanca, Salta, San Juan, etc, offering the full range of degrees, as well as specialist courses. There are also specialist institutions offering specialist technical subjects — for instance, leatherworking, winemaking, dance. A good source of information is UNESCO's *Study Abroad*.

Language of tuition Spanish.
Academic year April to November.
Best contacts for information
- Ministerio de Cultura y Educación, Paseo Colón 533, 1063 Buenos Aires (information for foreign students and details of institutions).
- Secretaría de Planeamiento de la Nación, 25 de mayo 459, 1002 Buenos Aires (grants and cultural exchange programmes).

Useful addresses
Student travel
AAA, Sarmiento 1262-7°A, Buenos Aires.
ATESA, Avda Santa Fe 1660-S 10, Buenos Aires 1060.

BAHRAIN

There are few possibilities for study in Bahrain; most opportunities for foreign students are directed towards nationals of other Gulf States.

Language of tuition Arabic and English.
Academic year October to June.
Best contacts for information
- Embassy of the State of Bahrain, 98 Gloucester Road, London SW7 4AU. Tel (01) 370 5132-5.
- Ministry of Education, Directorate of Cultural Affairs and Scholarships, PO Box 43, Manama.
- The Director of Student Affairs, University College of Arts, Science and Education, PO Box 1082P, Manama.

BENIN

Language of tuition French.
Academic year October to June.
Best contacts for information
- National University of Benin, PO Box 526, Cotonou.
- Embassy of the People's Republic of Benin, 87 avenue Victor Hugo, Paris 16. Tel (010 331) 4553 5045.

BOLIVIA

Language of tuition Spanish.

Academic year March to December.
Best contacts for information
● Comité Ejecutivo de Universidades de Bolivia, Avda Arce, esquina Pinilla, Casilla Postal 4722, La Paz (general information on study at Bolivian universities, academic requirements, grants available, etc).
● Bolivian Embassy, 106 Eaton Square, London SW1W 9AD. Tel (01) 235 4248 (visas).
● University of Bolivia, Mariscal José Ballivan, casilla 38, Trinidad-beni.

BRAZIL

Brazil has 65 universities, 45 of which are state-run and there are varied opportunities for Portuguese speakers, although nothing specifically directed at British students. There is a range of specialist courses at various institutions throughout Brazil listed in UNESCO's *Study Abroad*.

Language of tuition Portuguese.
Academic year March to December.
Best contacts for information
● Ministry of Foreign Affairs, Cultural Department, Esplanada dos Ministérios, 70 074 Brasilia DF (advice to foreigners on all aspects of studying in Brazil).
● Brazilian Embassy, 32 Green Street, London W1Y 3PD. Tel (01) 499 0877 (see their library, open Mondays to Fridays 10am to 1pm, and 3pm to 6pm).

Grants
The University of Itauna (UI), Rua Capitao Vicente 10, Edificio Maria Isabel, 35680 Itauna MG, offers grants for study over a range of subjects to students with a good command of Portuguese.

Postgraduate
The University of Sao Paulo offers scholarships to British graduates for 'well-defined research projects' in Science, Technology or Social Science to be carried out at the University. This takes the form of a monthly allowance, paid for a maximum of ten months, but does not include air fares. A month's intensive course in Portuguese can be provided if necessary. Apply to Coordenadoria de Atividades Culturais, Divisao de Difusao Cultural, Universidade de Sao Paulo,

Cidade Universitaria, Caixa Postal 8191, Sao Paulo, Brazil by July/August each year. Further information from the Brazilian Embassy.

Useful addresses

Student travel
Autec, Ave Presidente Vargas 583, Sala 1005, Rio de Janeiro.

BURKINA FASO

Language of tuition French.
Academic year October to July.
Best contacts for information
- University of Ouagadougou, PO Box 7021, Ouagadougou.
- Embassy of Burkina Faso, 16 place Guy d'Arezzo, 1060 Brussels, Belgium. Tel (010 322) 345 9911.

BURMA

Foreign students are not normally admitted to Burmese higher education institutions.

Language of tuition Burmese.
Academic year September to August.
Best contacts for information
- Ministry of Education, Rangoon.
- Embassy of the Socialist Republic of the Union of Burma, 19a Charles Street, Berkeley Square, London W1X 8ER. Tel (01) 499 8841.

BURUNDI

Language of tuition French.
Academic year October to June.
Best contacts for information
- University of Burundi, PO Box 1550, Bujumbura.
- Embassy of the Republic of Burundi, Square Marie Louise 46, 1040 Brussels, Belgium. Tel (010 322) 230 4535.

CAMEROON

Language of tuition French and English.
Academic year October to July.
Best contacts for information
- Service des Oeuvres Universitaires, PO Box 337, Yaoundé.
- University of Yaoundé, PO Box 1600, Yaoundé.
- Embassy of the Republic of Cameroon, 84 Holland Park, London W11 3SB. Tel (01) 727 0771.

CENTRAL AFRICAN REPUBLIC

Embassy of the Central African Republic, 29 boulevard Montmorency, 75016 Paris, France. Tel (010 331) 224 4256.

CHAD

Language of tuition French/Arabic
Academic year October to June.
Best contacts for information
- Ministry of Higher Education, Research and Grants, Njamena.
- Embassy of the Republic of Chad, boulevard Lambermont 52, 1030 Brussels, Belgium. Tel (010 322) 215 1975 (no Embassy in the UK).

CHILE

The main universities are the Catholic University of Chile (PUCCH) and the University of Chile (UCH), both in Santiago. Other universities are located in Concepción, Valparaíso and Valdivia. A full range of first degree and postgraduate courses is available.

Language of tuition Spanish.
Academic year March to December.
Best contacts for information
- Consejo de Rectores de Universidades Chilenas, Moneda 673, Santiago. Provides information on courses and degrees at Chilean universities. Publishes a booklet entitled *Información para estudiantes extranjeros*.
- Comisión Chilena de Cooperación Intelectual, Alameda Bernardo O'Higgins 1058, Santiago. A source of information

for foreigners wishing to study in Chile.

- Embassy of Chile (visas), 12 Devonshire Street, London W1N 2DS. Tel (01) 580 6392.

1st degree courses
Possible on a self-financing basis, for further details see contact addresses above.

Postgraduate
Again, see above. The Instituto de Estudios Internacionales of Chile University (casilla 14187, suc. 21, Santiago) publishes a guide entitled *Programa de Postgrado*. There are various grant schemes, listed in UNESCO's *Study Abroad*, which although not specifically for British students, are open to foreigners.

Language courses
Run by the Instituto de Lenguas of the University of Concepción.

CHINA

Since a period of stultification during the Cultural Revolution, education in China experienced a period of expansion and diversification, which means a degree of opportunity for foreigners as well as Chinese. Subjects most likely to be of interest are Chinese studies: language, literature and philosophy, also specialisms such as traditional Chinese medicine, or Chinese art and painting.

Language of tuition Chinese (Mandarin).
Academic year September to July.
Best contacts for information
- Embassy of the People's Republic of China, Education Section, 51 Drayton Green, West Ealing, London W13. Tel (01) 991 1649.

1st degree courses

Length Four years.

Contact
The Chinese Embassy Education Section (see above) can supply a *Directory of Specialities in Chinese Universities and Colleges Open to Foreign Students*. Further information on eligibility and how to apply is available from Bureau of Foreign Affairs, Ministry of

Education, No. 37 Da Mu Chang Hu Tong, Beijing.

Entrance requirements
Complete secondary education (A levels), plus at least two years
university education for so-called 'Advanced' courses, which last one
or two years only. In addition there are qualifying examinations for
courses in science, technology and medicine.

Cost Approx RMB2,000-RMB3,000 including board and lodging.

Postgraduate

Contact Chinese Embassy Education Section, as above.

Entrance requirements
Master's degree. 'Advanced' courses exist for which students with
a Bachelor's degree are eligible; see above.

Grants
There are a number of Chinese government scholarships available
each year through the British Council for postgraduates and 'Senior
Advanced Scholars'. The traditional fields of Chinese language,
history, philosophy and literature are now being expanded to include traditional Chinese medicine, fine arts and music. Some
knowledge of Mandarin is required. Grants are for eleven months,
and the British Council pays travel expenses. Apply by mid February
to British Council, OEAD, 65 Davies Street, London W1Y 2AA.
Tel (01) 499 8011.

Language courses

For courses in Chinese see also Singapore, Hong Kong and Taiwan.
One year advanced courses in Chinese language are run by various
institutions as listed in the *Directory of Specialities* (see above).
Shorter (6, 8 or 10 week) courses are held at a range of universities
and colleges throughout China. Write to Ministry of Education,
Foreign Affairs Bureau, No 37 Da Mu Chang Hu Tong, Beijing.

The **Society for Anglo-Chinese Understanding** (SACU), 152
Camden High Street, London NW1 0NE, tel (01) 482 4292, offers
the chance to attend three or four courses in Chinese at the People's
University in Beijing and in Harbin, handling booking, visas and
travel arrangements. The Society can also arrange specialist group
tours and study visits.

Other useful addresses
Embassy of the People's Republic of China, 49-51 Portland Place, London W1N 3AH. Tel (01) 636 9375.
Great Britain-China Centre, 15 Belgrave Square, London SW1X 8PG. Tel (01) 235 9216.
China National Tourist Office, 4 Glentworth Street, London NW1. Tel (01) 935 9427.

COLOMBIA

There are several universities in Bogotá, including the National University of Colombia; other universities are to be found in Bucaramanga, Popayán, Medellín and Cartagena.

Language of tuition Spanish.
Academic year February to November.
Best contacts for information
- Centro de Documentación, Oficina de Información Académica, Instituto Colombiano de Crédito Educativo y Estudios Técnicos en el Exterior (ICETEX), Carrera 3 no. 18-24, Apartado aéreo 5735, Bogotá (information on university courses).
- Instituto Colombiano para el Fomento de la Educación Superior (ICFES), Calle 17 no. 3-40, Apartado aéreo 6319, Bogotá. Sets entrance exams, and publishes a useful guide, *Directorio de Estudios Superiores en Colombia.*
- Colombian Embassy (visas), Flat 3a, 3 Hans Crescent, London SW1X 0LR. Tel (01) 589 9177.

Language courses
Run by the Pontificia Universidad Javeriana, Carrera 7 no. 40-62, Bogotá.

CONGO

Embassy of the People's Republic of the Congo, 37 bis rue Paul Valéry, Paris 16, France. Tel (010 331) 4500 6057.

COSTA RICA

A fairly complete range of courses is run by the national university and other institutions — full fees are payable.

Language of tuition Spanish.
Academic year March to November.
Best contacts for information
- Universidad de Costa Rica. Has various offices: for information about courses and accommodation, contact the 'Oficina de Bienestar Estudiantil'; for exchanges and visits, contact the 'Oficiana de Asuntos Internacionales'. The postal address is Ciudad Universitaria 'Rodrigo Facio', San José.
- Costa Rican Embassy, 93 Star Street, London W2. Tel (01) 723 9630.

Language courses
Organised by the Escuela de Filología of the University of Costa Rica; see above.

Useful addresses

Student travel
OTEC, Paseo Estudiantes, PO Box 323, San José 1002.

CUBA

Education is free, so there is a careful official control over foreigners allowed into the country to take advantage of it. Foreign students are generally admitted under international exchange programmes: there are none specifically aimed at British students.

Language of tuition Spanish.
Academic year September to July.
Best contacts for information
- Ministerio de Educación Superior, Calle 23 esquina a F. Vedado, Habana 4, Ciudad de La Habana.
- Embassy of the Republic of Cuba, 167 High Holborn, London WC1. Tel (01) 240 2488.

DJIBOUTI

Embassy of the Republic of Djibouti, 26 rue Emile Ménier, 75116 Paris, France. Tel (010 33) 4727 4922.

ECUADOR

Language of tuition Spanish.
Academic year October to June in the mountain region. May to December in the coastal region.
Best contacts for information
- Ministerio de Educación y Cultura, Departamento de Asuntos y Convenios Internacionales, Quito.
- Secretariado General Permanente del Consejo Nacional de Educación Superior, Santa Prisca 269, Quito.
- Embassy of Ecuador, Flat 3b, Hans Crescent, London SW1X 0LS. Tel (01) 584 1367.

Useful addresses

Student travel
CEPTEJ, Brasil no. 1400 y P. Moncayo, PO Box 10610, Guayaquil.

EGYPT

Language of tuition Arabic with some English.
Academic year October to June.
Best contacts for information
- British Council, 192 Sharia el Nil, Agouza, Cairo. Tel (010 202) 345 3281-4.

Visiting studentships
The American University in Cairo, PO Box 2511, Cairo, runs a **Year Abroad Programme** open to all nationalities. It offers a wide range of subject areas, including Arabic language, Middle Eastern studies, Egyptology etc as well as run-of-the-mill subjects. Their prospectus ('catalog') is also available from The American University in Cairo, 866 United Nations Plaza, New York NY 10017, USA. Some scholarships are available for graduates.

Language courses
Courses in Arabic for foreigners are run by the following:
American University of Cairo, 113 Sharia Kasr El Ainri, Cairo.
One year courses, as described above, and also summer courses.
Dept of Wafidin, 2 Darih Saad Street, Monira, Cairo.
Helwan University, Faculty of Languages, Al-Alsun, Cairo.
International Language Institute, Mahmoud Azmy Street, Madinet

el Sahafeyeen, Cairo. See also the International House head office in the UK (p.29) for further details.

Other useful addresses

Supreme Council for Islamic Affairs, 9 Nabatat Street, Garden City, Cairo.

Arab League Educational, Cultural and Scientific Organisation, 109 Tahrir Street, Dokki, Giza.

Embassy of the Arab Republic of Egypt, 26 South Street, London W1Y 8EL. Tel (01) 499 2401.

Egypt Tourist Information Office, 168 Piccadilly, London W1. Tel (01) 493 5282.

EL SALVADOR

The National University (Universidad de El Salvador, Ciudad Universitaria, San Salvador) is presently closed more often than not due to the political crisis; this has however given rise to the establishment of a whole clutch of private universities.

Language of tuition Spanish.
Academic year February to November.
Best contacts for information
● Embassy of El Salvador, Flat 9, Welbeck House, 62 Welbeck Street, London W1. Tel (01) 486 8182.
● Ministerio de Educación, Oficina de Relaciones Internacionales, Edificio Biblioteca Nacional, San Salvador.

EQUATORIAL GUINEA

Embassy of the Republic of Equatorial Guinea, 6 rue Alfred de Vigny, 75008 Paris, France. Tel (010 331) 766 4433.

ETHIOPIA

Academic year October to June.
Best contacts for information
● Addis Ababa University, PO Box 1176, Addis Ababa.
● Embassy of the Provisional Military Government of Socialist Ethiopia, 17 Prince's Gate, London SW7 1PZ. Tel (01) 589 7212.

GABON

Language of tuition French/English.
Academic year October to June.
Best contacts for information
● Omar Bongo University, PO Box 13131, Libreville.
● Embassy of the Republic of Gabon, 48 Kensington Court, London W8. Tel (01) 879 0369.

GUATEMALA

Language of tuition Spanish.
Academic year January to November.
Best contacts for information
● Ministerio de Educación Pública, Departamento de Coordinación con Organismos Internacionales, Palacio Nacional, Guatemala.

Language courses
Summer schools in Spanish language and literature and anthropology are organized by the Faculty of Humanities of the Universidad de San Carlos de Guatemala. Apply to the Departamento de Registro y Estadística, Ciudad Universitaria, zona 12, Guatemala.

GUINEA

Embassy of the Republic of Guinea, 24 rue de Emile Ménier, 75116 Paris, France. Tel (010 331) 553 7225.

HAITI

Language of tuition French.
Best contacts for information
● Embassy of the Republic of Haiti, 55 Park Lane, Suite 5, London W1Y 3DH. Tel (01) 409 3115.

HONDURAS

Language of tuition Spanish.
Academic year January to November.

Best contacts for information
- Ministerio de Educación Pública, Dirección General de Planea-miento y Reforma Educativa, 1a calle, entre 2a y 4a Avenidas, Comayagüela, DC.
- Universidad Nacional Autónoma de Honduras, Ciudad Univer-sitaria, Tegucigalpa DC.
- Embassy of Honduras, 47 Manchester Street, London W1M 5PB. Tel (01) 486 3380.

Language courses
Apply to Department de Letras y Lenguas, Universidad Nacional Autónoma de Honduras, as above.

HONG KONG

Best areas of study Chinese languages, Asian Studies.
Language of tuition English (University of Hong Kong); also Chinese at Chinese University of Hong Kong and Hong Kong Polytechnic.
Academic year September to August.
Best contacts for information
- British Council, 20th Floor, Commercial Building, 253-261 Hennessy Road, Wanchai.
- Chinese University of Hong Kong, Shatin, New Territories.
- University of Hong Kong, Pokfulam Road.
- Hong Kong Polytechnic, Yuk Choi Road, Hung Hom, Kowloon.
- Hong Kong Baptist College, 224 Waterloo Road, Kowloon.

Postgraduate
Grants for postgraduate study are available through the Common-wealth Scholarship and Fellowship plan; see p.51.

Language courses
A variety of language courses, for beginners upwards, in Mandarin Chinese or Cantonese, and lasting from ten weeks to three years, is run at the New Asia Yale-in-China Language Centre, at the Chinese University of Hong Kong, Shatin, New Territories.

An International Asian Studies Programme is also run by the same department; it lasts one semester or a whole academic year, and is open to graduates and undergraduates of any nationality.

The Language Centre of the University of Hong Kong (Pokfulam Road) also offers a range of courses leading to Diplomas and Certificates in Cantonese or Mandarin.

Useful addresses

Student travel
HKSTB, 8/F Tai Sang Bank Building, 130-132 Des Voeux Road Central, Hong Kong.

INDONESIA

Language of tuition Bahasa Indonesia.
Academic year July to June.
Best contacts for information
● Indonesian Embassy, 38 Grosvenor Square, London W1X 9AD. Tel (01) 499 7661.

Language courses
Courses in Indonesian language and culture lasting one semester (beginning July) or more, are run by the Senata Dharma Teacher Training Institute, Jalan Gejayan, Mrican, Tromol Pos 29, Yogyakarta.

Other useful addresses
Indonesian Tourist Information Centre, 70 New Bond Street, London W1. Tel (01) 629 0862.

IRAN

There are obvious difficulties as regards study in Iran due to the political situation. At the time of writing it is extremely doubtful whether potential students would be able to obtain a visa.

Language of tuition Persian (Farsi).
Academic year September to June.
Best contacts for information
● University of Teheran, Avenue Enghelabe, Teheran.
● Ministry of Higher Education and Culture, PO Box 54/552, Ayatullah Beheshti Street, Delapazir Crossroads, Teheran.

IRAQ

At the present time it is very doubtful whether entry visas would be granted to potential students.

Language of tuition Mainly Arabic.
Academic year September to June.
Best contacts for information
● Ministry of Higher Education, Directorate-General of Cultural Affairs, Baghdad.
● Embassy of the Republic of Iraq, 27 Prince's Gate, London SW7 1PX. Tel (01) 584 8101-8.

ISRAEL

Israel offers a wide range of study possibilities, being well set up for receiving (mainly) Jewish students from all over the world. You don't *have* to be Jewish to take advantage of these, although you will obviously need to have a certain sympathy towards Jewish culture.

Language of tuition Hebrew, with some English, see below.
Academic year October to June.
Best contacts for information
● Council for Higher Education, PO Box 4037, 12 Hanassi Street, Jerusalem 91040. Can supply a useful booklet entitled *Higher Education in Israel: A Guide for Overseas Students,* which gives full details of all the study possibilities referred to below, with lists of institutions, courses etc.

1st degree courses
Length Three years in a university, four in colleges. Some professionally-oriented studies may take longer.

Contact
Each institution, or alternatively the various Aliyah Centres in the UK, which can transfer applications to the relevant authorities in Israel:

Balfour House, 741 Finchley High Road, London N12 0BQ. Tel (01) 446 1477.
Mamlock House, 142 Bury Old Road, Manchester M8 6HD. Tel (061) 740 2864.
43 Queen Square, Glasgow. Tel (041) 423 7379.

Entrance requirements
Applicants' qualifications are examined by special committees operating in each university institution. Generally two 'A' levels plus three GCSEs are accepted as the minimum requirement; notarised photocopies of the certificates must be sent to the university. In addition there is an entrance exam (facilities exist for sitting this outside Israel) which is intended as a test of cognitive ability and may be taken in English. Students with an insufficient knowledge of Hebrew must take a language course (see below) before commencing studies.

Cost/grants
Costs are about £1,000 excluding living and accommodation expenses. Funding is not generally available for overseas students, however, although the Student Authority grants financial aid to temporary residents holding an A/1 type visa. For information about visas contact the Israeli Embassy in London, 2 Palace Green, London W8 4QB. Tel (01) 937 8050.

Postgraduate
Contact As for first degrees above.

Entrance requirements
BA degree plus knowledge of Hebrew. Depending on the course followed students may be required to take supplementary courses alongside or prior to postgraduate work.

Grants
The Israeli government offers 30 scholarships annually to foreign graduates for study or research in any field at one of the following:

Hebrew University of Jerusalem
Israel Institute of Technology, Haifa
Tel Aviv University
Ramat Aviv-Bar-Ilan University
Ramat Gan Weizmann Institute of Science, Rehovot

The scholarship takes the form of a monthly allowance paid over nine (sometimes eleven) months, plus free tuition, but excluding travel expenses. Apply to Israeli Embassy, Counsellor for Cultural Affairs, 2 Palace Green, London W8 4QB tel (01) 937 8050, normally by 31st December. For further information in Israel apply to Ministry of Education & Culture, 34 Shivtei Yisrael Street,

Jerusalem.

For post-doctoral research fellowships in scientific fields at the Weizmann Institute of Science, apply to the Dean of Feinberg Graduate School, Weizmann Institute, Rehovot 76100.

For details of other scholarships awarded for specific fields of study, see UNESCO's *Study Abroad.*

Visiting studentships

The Hebrew University of Jerusalem runs a one-year program(me) For foreign students which is built around a core of courses given in English. It mainly attracts US or Canadian students, whose universities accept the credit earned towards a degree. Most emphasis is on Jewish, Israeli or Middle Eastern Studies, but there is also scope for students with interests in archaeology, social work or urban studies. Apply to Hebrew University of Jerusalem, Rothberg School for Overseas Students, Goldsmith Building, Mount Scopus, Jerusalem 91905.

Language courses

Several options are available for people wishing to learn Hebrew or improve on their existing knowledge.

Intensive language courses **(ulpanim)** are held at universities before the start of the academic year, for students who need to improve their proficiency before embarking on a course of study.

One-year preparatory program(me)s **(mechinot)** are available for students who need a more thorough grounding in Jewish studies and Hebrew language before starting their course.

A five-month 'Academic Absorption Program for Advanced Students' known as **TAKA** is held at the University of Haifa, designed for students who have already completed at least one year of university education.

Kibbutz ulpanim combine the study of Hebrew with work on a kibbutz and generally last four or five months. Detailed information about this scheme is contained in a publication entitled *Kibbutz Ulpan,* available free from Aliyah Centres (see p.148) or from Ministry of Immigrant Absorption, Publications Dept, PO Box 13061, 91130 Jerusalem.

Summer courses in Hebrew and Jewish/Middle Eastern studies are organised by the Hebrew University of Jerusalem, Rothberg School for Overseas Students, Goldsmith Building, Mt Scopus, Jerusalem 91905. Two scholarships a year are offered for teachers of Hebrew in Britain to attend these courses. Apply to Israeli Em-

bassy, Counsellor for Cultural Affairs, 2 Palace Green, London W8
4QB, tel (01) 937 8050, for details.

Joint programmes/special schemes

There is a variety of International Courses in specialist subjects including agriculture, arts & design, Holy Land studies, public health,
labour studies, medicine, and community development, listed in
Study Abroad (see p.174).

Yeshiva studies

A variety of **yeshivot** offer courses in Jewish thought and practice
lasting from two weeks to several years. Many beginners' courses
are held in English. Write to Publications Dept, Ministry of Immigrant Absorption, PO Box 13061, 91130 Jerusalem, for the
booklet *Yeshiva Studies in Israel*.

Other useful addresses

Israel Association for International Co-operation, PO Box 13006,
Jerusalem.

National Union of Israeli Students, Student Centre, Hebrew
University, Jerusalem.

Israel Government, Tourist Office, 18 Great Marlborough Street,
London W1. Tel (01) 434 3651.

Embassy of Israel Consular Section, 2 Palace Green, London W8.
Tel (01) 937 8050.

Student travel

ISSTA, 109 Ben Yehuda Street, Tel Aviv.
Youth Travel Bureau, Israel Youth Hostels Association, 3 Dorot
Rishonim Street, PO Box 1075, Jerusalem 91009, tel (010 9722)
221648 or 232430.

IVORY COAST

Language of tuition French.
Academic year October to June.
Best contacts for information
- Service de la Scolarité, University of Abidjan, Abidjan.
- Embassy of the Republic of the Ivory Coast, 2 Upper Belgrave
  Street, London SW1X 8BJ. Tel (01) 235 6991.

JAPAN

There are good opportunities in Japan both in state-maintained and private institutions; eighty per cent of university education is private, and there are many private institutions offering language courses.

Best fields of study
Japanese language, Asian studies, science and technology. Apart from these, Japan, as a highly developed society, has schools catering for all sorts of specialised areas of interest: kendo, judo, doll making, flower arranging, music and art — even schools which can instruct you in the art of the tea ceremony!

Language of tuition Japanese.
Academic year April to March.
Best contacts for information
● Japan Information Centre, Embassy of Japan, 9 Grosvenor Square, London W1X 9LB. Tel (01) 493 6030.
● Student Exchange Division, Science and International Affairs Bureau, Ministry of Education, Science and Culture, 3-2-2 Kasumigaseki, Chiyoda-ku, Tokyo.

1st degree courses

Length
Mainly four years. Some junior colleges offer two or three year courses in liberal arts — mainly for women.

Contact
Universities themselves. The Japan Information Centre (see above) can provide addresses.

Entrance requirements
12 years' education is the general requirement, but see individual institutions for further orientation.

Cost/grants
Expensive. About 1 million yen (£5,000) for fees, plus a similar amount for rooms, plus books, living expenses etc. This would have to be self-funded as grants are not generally available.

Postgraduate

Contact
Individual institutions. See Japan Information Centre (above) for addresses.

Entrance requirements
16 years' formal education. See individual institutions for further details.

Grants
A number of short and long term awards are available at postgraduate, post-doctorate and senior scientist levels. A list is available from the British Council in Tokyo, 2-Kagurazaka 1-Chome, Shinjuku-ku, tel (010 813) 235 8031, or from the Japanese Information Centre (see above). Of most interest are the two to three year Japanese Government (Mombusho) Scholarships for any area of postgraduate study. No knowledge of Japanese is required to apply, but those who are offered an award must be willing to spend six months at a language school in Japan before taking it up. Applications for these should be made through the Japan Information Centre.

Language courses
A wide range of language courses is available for foreigners wishing to learn Japanese in Japan. Many universities run preparatory language courses, usually of a year's duration, for non-Japanese students intending to take up university places. These include, for example The Japanese Language School, International Students Institute, 3-22-7 Kitashijuku, Shinjuku-ku, Tokyo; its course costs approximately 500,000 yen (£2,400) for the year, with (dormitory) accommodation extra. A full list is available from the Japanese Information Centre.

The Centre for Japanese Studies of Nanzan University, 18 Yamazato-cho, Showa-ku, Nagoya 466, runs not only language courses, but courses (in English) in oriental arts such as calligraphy, flower arrangements, Chinese black ink painting etc, as well as a wide range of lectures on Japanese Studies.

For shorter language courses choose one of the many private language schools, which are only too keen to advertise their services. Again, the Japan Information Centre will put you on the right track.

Visiting studentships

Waseda University, 6-1 Nishi-Waseda 1-chome, Shinjuku-ku, Tokyo 160, runs a special one-year Study Abroad Programme, in English, concentrating on Asian Studies and Japanese language. It is open to both undergraduates and postgraduates.

Special schemes

The Kansai University of Foreign Studies, Office of International Studies, 16-1 Kitakatahoko-cho, Kirakata City, Osaka 573, offers **Teaching Assistantships** to native English speakers with university-level education. These may be combined with the study of Japanese on their Asian Studies Programme.

Welfare

Advice and assistance, including details of medical care, can be obtained from the Association of International Education of Japan (AIEJ), 4-5-29 Komaba, Meguro-ku, Tokyo.

Other useful addresses

For those interested in martial arts: The Japan Karate Association, 1-6-1 Ebisu Nishi, Shibuya-ku, Tokyo.

Japan National Tourist Organisation, 167 Regent Street, London W1. Tel (01) 734 9638.

Student travel
NFUCA, Sanshin-Hokusei Building, 2nd Floor, 2-4-9 Yoyogi, Shibuya-ku, Tokyo 151.

JORDAN

Language of tuition Arabic and English (both essential).
Academic year September to May/June.
Best contacts for information
● Embassy of the Hashemite Kingdom of Jordan, 6 Upper Phillimore Gardens, London W8 7HB. Tel (01) 937 3685.

Grants

For details of scholarships offered by the Jordanian Ministry of Education, try applying to:
University of Jordan, Amman.
Yarmouk University, Irbid.

Language courses
Arabic language courses for foreign students are offered at the Yarmouk University Language Centre, Irbid, and at the Arabic Dept, Faculty of Arts, University of Jordan, Amman.

Joint programmes/special schemes
A two month training programme can be arranged through the International Association for the Exchange of Students for Technical Experience (IAESTE); it is open to 3rd and 4th year engineering students attending foreign universities, and is held each year at the University of Jordan. Applications should be made through the Faculty of Engineering and Technology, University of Jordan, Amman.

KOREA

Some worthwhile opportunities are available for those interested in Korean Studies.
Language of tuition Korean.
Academic year March to February.
Best contacts for information
● Ministry of Education, Overseas Resident Education Division, 77 Sejon-ro-Jongro-gu, Seoul.
● Korean Institute of International Educational Exchange, 25-1 Sam Chung Dong Chong-ro Gu, Seoul.
● Embassy of the Republic of Korea, 4 Palace Gate, London W8 5NF. Tel (01) 581 0247.

1st degree courses

Length Normally four years.

Contact Ministry of Education; see above.

Entrance requirements 12 years' schooling. Knowledge of Korean essential.

Grants
Scholarships or fee waivers may be awarded to foreign nationals with good academic backgrounds and knowledge of Korean. Apply direct to the following institutions:

Keimyung University, Daegu.

King Sejong University, Gunja-Dong, Sungdong-ku, Seoul 133.

Kon-Kuk University, Office of the President, 93 Mojin-dong, Sungdong-ku, Seoul.

Kyungpook National University, Bureau of Student Affairs, 370 San Kyukdong, Puk-gu, Daegu 635.

Yeungnam University, Office of International Affairs, Gyongsan 632.

Postgraduate

Contact As above.

Entrance requirements
First degree, plus Master's degree for Doctorates. Knowledge of Korean.

Grants See above. Also the following, for Korean studies only:

Academy of Korean Studies, Graduate School, 50 Unjung-dong, Seongnam-si, Gyeonggi-do 130-17.

International Cultural Foundation, 185 Kahwe-dong, Chongro-ku, Seoul.

Korea University, 1 Anam-dong, Sungbuk-ku, Seoul.

Visiting studentships
Yonsei University, 134 Sinchon-Dong, Seodaemun-Gu, Seoul 120, offers a Junior Year Abroad programme (designed for American students but open to other English speakers who have completed at least one year at university); it concentrates mainly on Korean and Asian studies.

One year courses in Korean and Asian studies, open to English-speaking graduates or undergraduates, are run by the Ewha Women's University, International Education Institute, Seoul.

Language courses
The Ewha Women's University, Seoul, offers both year long courses and six week summer courses in Korean; it also offers an International Co-Ed summer school in Asian Studies with scholarships available for second-time participants.

A year long course in Korean, with teaching in English, is run by the Language Research Institute, Education and Training Division, Seoul National University, San 56-1 Shinlim-Dong, Kwanak-ku,

Seoul 151.

Joint programmes/special schemes
Teaching assistantships in English language are available to graduates aged under 30, with knowledge of Korean, at the Chung-Ang University, International Education Dept, 221 Huksuk-dong, Dongjak-ku, Seoul 1516. Candidates selected are eligible for free tuition at the university in addition to their salary.

Useful addresses
Korea National Tourist Corporation, Vogue House, Hanover Square, London W1. Tel (01) 409 2100.

Student travel
KIYSES, Rm.504-5 YMCA Building, 9, 2-Ka Changro, Chongro-Ku, Seoul.

KUWAIT

Kuwait University (Foreign Students Office, PO Box 5969, Kaldia) offers a range of courses. Foreign students with full secondary education may be admitted.

Language of tuition Arabic and English.
Academic year September to June.
Best contacts for information
● Kuwait University (see above); ask for their 'General Catalogue'.
● Embassy of the State of Kuwait, 45-46 Queen's Gate, London SW7. Tel (01) 589 5433.

Language courses
Run at Kuwait University Language Centre, PO Box 5486, Safat. One year scholarships are available for non-Arabic speaking graduate Moslems aged under 28.

LEBANON

At time of writing the civil war makes study in Lebanon an extremely difficult proposition.

Language of tuition Arabic/French/English

Academic year October to July.

Best contacts for information
- Lebanon University, Central Administration, Place du Musée National, Beirut.
- The American University of Beirut, PO Box 236, Beirut.
- Lebanese Embassy, 21 Kensington Palace Gardens, London W8 4QM. Tel (01) 229 7265.

LIBERIA

Embassy of the Republic of Liberia, 2 Pembridge Place, London W2. Tel (01) 221 1036.

LIBYA

It would be extremely difficult for British students to obtain permission to study in Libya, due to the rift in diplomatic relations.
Language of tuition Arabic (and English in the science faculties).
Academic year October to June.

Best contacts for information
- Department of Cultural Relations, Secretariat of State for Education, Tripoli.
- Rectorate of Qaar University, Benghazi.
- Rectorate of Fatih University, Tripoli.

MADAGASCAR

Language of tuition French
Academic year October to June.
Best contacts for information
- Madagascar University, PO Box 566, Antananarivo.
- Embassy of the Republic of Madagascar, 4 avenue Raphael, 75016 Paris. Tel (010 33) 4504 6211 (no Embassy in the UK).

MALI

Embassy of the Republic of Mali, 487 Avenue Molière, 1060 Brussels, Belgium. Tel (010 322) 345 7432.

MALTA

Language of tuition English.
Academic year February to July and September to February.

Useful addresses
University of Malta, Msida, Malta.
Malta High Commission, 16 Kensington Square, London W8 5HH. Tel (01) 938 1712.
Education Office, Lascaris, Valletta.

Student travel
NSTF-STF, 220 St Paul's Street, Valletta...

MAURITANIA

Embassy of the Islamic Republic of Mauritania, 5 rue de Montevideo, 75016 Paris, France. Tel (010 33) 4504 8854.

MEXICO

There are good possibilities for study in Mexico at undergraduate or postgraduate level in both public and private sectors, and a generally positive attitude towards international contacts seems to prevail.

Language of tuition Spanish.
Academic year September to June.
Best contacts for information
● Secretaría de Educación Pública, Dirección General de Relaciones Internacionales, Brasil 31, México 1 DF, CP 06029. General information for foreign students wishing to study in Mexico.
● Secretaría de Relaciones Exteriores, Dirección General de Asuntos Culturales, Avda Ricardo Flores Magón 1, México 3 DF, CP 06995. Exchanges and bilateral schemes.
● Consejo Nacional de Ciencia y Tecnología (CONACYT), Dirección de Orientación y Capacitación de la Dirección Adjunta de Formación de Recursos Humanos, Circuito Cultural, Centro Cultural Universitario, Ciudad Universitaria, Acceso 'B', planta baja, 04515 México DF. For information on study in scientific

and technical subjects at under and postgraduate levels.
- Universidad Nacional Autónoma de México (UNAM), Ciudad Universitaria, 04510 Mexico DF.
- Mexican Embassy, 8 Halkin Street, London SW1 7DW. Tel (01) 235 6393.

Grants

The following institutions offer grants to British postgraduate students with a knowledge of Spanish for study or research at a Mexican institution for one academic year:

National Autonomous University of Mexico (UNAM — as above)
Ministry of Foreign Affairs
Ministry of Public Education

For all these, apply through the Mexican Embassy in London, but *at the same time make contact with the institution where you wish to study in Mexico.* You can get information on these from any of the addresses given above.

Similar grants, but which include air fares as well, are offered by CONACYT (see above), in certain subjects only. For these you must apply to the British Council, OEAD, 65 Davies Street, London W1Y 2AA.

Various other Mexican institutions offer grants under other conditions for specific areas of study: full details of these appear in UNESCO's *Study Abroad.*

Visiting studentships

A number of institutions run courses for visiting students, under the guise of 'Junior Year Abroad Programs' aimed mostly at US students. They include: Universidad Autónoma de Guadalajara, Paso de las Aguilas 7000, Lomas del Valle 3a sección, Guadalajara (Jalisco).

Universidad Iberoamericana, Centro Internacional, Cerro de las Torres 395, Campestre Churubusco CP 04200, México 21 DF.

Universidad Nacional Autónoma de México, Centro de Enseñanza para Extranjeros, Apartado Postal 70-391, Ciudad Universitaria, 04510 Mexico DF.

Universidad Internacional de México AC, La Otra Banda No. 40, Col. Tizapan, Del A Obregon, 01090 México DF (associate campus of the University of San Diego, California).

Language courses

These are run by both public and private institutions, including the following:

Academia Hispano Americana, Mesones 4, San Miguel de Allende (GT), 37700, tel (010 52 465) 20349. Courses all the year round in Spanish language, literature and history.

Centro de Idiomas del Consejo Nacional de Ciencia y Tecnología (CONACYT), Circuito Cultural, Centro Cultural Universitario, Ciudad Universitaria, Acceso 'B', planta baja, 04515 México.

Instituto Allende, San Miguel de Allende (Guanajuato), CP 37700. Tel (010 52 465) 20190. Open throughout the year, also runs courses in art and crafts.

Instituto Mexicano-Norteamericano de Relaciones Culturales, Hamburgo 115, Mexico 6 DF, CP 06600. Runs 3 week courses throughout the year.

Universidad Autónoma de Guadalajara, Avda Patria 1201, Lomas del Valle, 3ra sección, CP 44100, apartado postal 1-440, Guadalajara (Jalisco). Various types of course are offered.

Universidad Nacional Autónoma de México, Departamento para Estudiantes Extranjeros, Ciudad Universitaria, México 20 DF (various programmes).

Universidad Autónoma del Estado de Morelos, c/Universidad, Chamilpa, Cuernavaca. Summer courses June-October in Spanish language, Mexican history, Hispanic literature, anthropology etc.

Instituto Cultural Mexicano Norteamericano de Jalisco, AC, Tolsá 300, Guadalajara (Jalisco). Runs four and six week courses throughout the year.

Useful addresses

Student travel
CREA, Oxtopulo no. 40, Col Oxtopulco, Universidad CP 04310, México DF.
SE-TEJ-MEX, Hamburgo 273, Col Juarez, Mexico City 6, DF.
Mexico Ministry of Tourism, 7 Cork Street, London W1. Tel (01) 734 1058.

MONGOLIA

Embassy of the Mongolian People's Republic, 7 Kensington Court, London W8 5DL. Tel (01) 937 0150.

Postgraduate scholarships
A number of postgraduate scholarships lasting from two to six

months are available at the University of Ulan Bator. Candidates must have a well defined study or research project and a working knowledge of Mongolian. Apply to the British Council, OEAD, 65 Davies Street, London W1Y 2AA. Tel (01) 499 8011.

MOROCCO

Language of tuition Arabic and, in some universities, French.
Academic year October to June.
Best contacts for information
● Institut Universitaire de la Recherche Scientifique (IURS), Rabat. Publishes information on the academic situation in Morocco.
● Ministère de l'education nationale et de la formation des cadres, Place de la Victoire, Rabat.
● Embassy of the Kingdom of Morocco, 49 Queens Gate Gardens, London SW7 5NE. Tel (01) 581 5001-4.
● Moroccan Tourist Office, 174 Regent Street, London W1. Tel (01) 437 0073.

NICARAGUA

Language of tuition Spanish.
Academic year May to February.
Best contacts for information
● Ministerio de Educación Pública, Dirección de Extensión Cultural, Managua.
● Universidad Nacional Autónoma de Nicaragua, Leon.
● Universidad Centroamericana, apartado 69, Managua.
● Embassy of Nicaragua, 8 Gloucester Road, London SW7 4PP. Tel (01) 584 4365.
● Progressive Tours, 12 Porchester Place, London W2 2BS. Tel (01) 262 1676.

Student travel
TUR-NICA, Plaza España 250, PO Box 3580, Managua.

NIGER

Language of tuition French/English.

Academic year October to June.
Best contacts for information
- University of Niamey, PO Box 237 or 10896, Niamey.
- Embassy of the Republic of Niger, 154 rue de Longchamp, 75116 Paris. Tel (010 331) 504 8060 (no Embassy in the UK).

PAKISTAN

Language of tuition English/Urdu. In some cases a regional language.
Academic year September to August.
Best contacts for information
- Ministry of Education, Islamabad. See also Education Offices in each of the four regions (Lahore — Punjab; Karachi — Sind; Quetta — Baluchistan; Pershawar — North West Frontier).
- Embassy of Pakistan, 35 Lowndes Square, London SW1X 9JN. Tel (01) 235 2044.

PANAMA

Language of tuition Spanish.
Academic year April to December.
Best contacts for information
- Ministerio de Educación, Unidad de Relaciones Internacionales, Apartado 2440, Panamá.
- Instituto para la Formación y Aprovechamiento de Recursos Humanos, Centro de Información y Documentación (IFARHU/CIDI), Avda 7a España, edificio Diorvett Internacional, apartado 6337, Panamá 5.
- Embassy of the Republic of Panama, 2nd Floor, Eagle House, 109 Jermyn Street, London SW1. Tel (01) 930 1591.

PARAGUAY

Language of tuition Spanish.
Best contacts for information
- Embassy of Paraguay, Braemar Lodge, Cornwall Gardens, London SW7 4AQ. Tel (01) 937 1253.

PERU

Language of tuition Spanish.

Academic year April to December.
Best contacts for information
● Ministerio de Educación Pública, Parque Universitario s/n, Lima 1.
● Peruvian Embassy, 52 Sloane Street, London SW1X 9SP. Tel (01) 235 1917.

Student travel
INTEJ, Av San Martín 240, Lima 4.

PHILIPPINES

A range of Philippine institutions offer courses in various fields (especially education and commerce) which are open to foreign students.

Language of tuition English, also Spanish and Tagalog (Filipino).
Academic year June to March.
Best contacts for information
● Dept of Education and Culture, Arroceros Street, Ermita, Manila.
● University of the Philippines, Diliman, Quezon City.
● Embassy of the Philippines, 9a Palace Green, London W8 4QE. Tel (01) 937 1600/09.
● Philippines Dept of Tourism, 199 Piccadilly, London W1, tel (01) 438 3481.

Student travel
YSTAPHIL, Suite 104, Marietta Apartments, 1200 J Bocobo Street, Ermita Metro, Manila.

RWANDA

Embassy of the Rwanda Republic, 1 avenue des Fleurs, 1150 Brussels, Belgium. Tel (010 322) 169 0702.

SAUDI ARABIA

Few possibilities — foreign students are admitted from 'Arab, Moslem and friendly countries'.

Best areas of study Petroleum and minerals, Islamic Studies and Arabic.

Language of tuition Arabic, except at the University of Petroleum, where instruction is in English.

Academic year September to May.

Best contacts for information

- Ministry of Higher Education, Office of the Deputy Minister for Technical Affairs and the Secretary General of Supreme Council of Universities, Riyadh.
- Royal Embassy of Saudi Arabia, 30 Belgrave Square, London SW1X 8QB. Tel (01) 235 0831.

SENEGAL

Dakar is the seat of the African Cultural Institute, comprising Benin, Comores, Congo, Central African Republic, Ivory Coast, Gabon, Ghana, Guinea, Burkina Faso, Mauritius, Mauritania, Niger, Rwanda, Senegal, Seychelles, Chad, Sierra Leone, Togo and Zambia.

Language of tuition French.

Academic year October to June.

Best contacts for information

- Overseas Students' Office, Direction de Formation Permanente (DFP), 71 avenue Peytavin, PO Box 11027, CD annex, Dakar.
- ICA (African Cultural Institute), 14 avenue du Président Lamine Gueye, PO Box 01, Dakar.
- Embassy of the Republic of Senegal, 11 Phillimore Gardens, London W8 7QG. Tel (01) 937 0925/6.

SOMALIA

Embassy of the Somali Democratic Republic, 60 Portland Place, London W1N 3DG. Tel (01) 580 7140.

SRI LANKA

Language of tuition Sinhala, Tamil and English.

Academic year January to December.

Best contacts for information

- Director General of Education, Ministry of Education, Malay

Street, Colombo 2.
- High Commission for the Democratic Socialist Republic of Sri Lanka, 13 Hyde Park Gardens, London W2 2LX. Tel (01) 262 1841.

SUDAN

Language of tuition English. Arabic for the Islamic University of Omdurman.
Academic year July to March.
Best contacts for information
- Dept of Foreign Cultural Relations, National Council for Higher Education, PO Box 2081, Khartoum.
- Admissions Office, University of Khartoum, Khartoum.
- Embassy of the Democratic Republic of the Sudan, 3 Cleveland Row, London SW1A. Tel (01) 839 8080.

SYRIA

Syrian universities do admit foreign students. However, since Britain severed diplomatic relations with Syria on 24th October 1986, it is extremely doubtful whether British students would be accepted.

Language of tuition Arabic.
Academic year October to June.
Best contacts for information
- Ministry of Higher Education, Damascus.

TAIWAN

Language courses
Three month courses in Mandarin at different levels (including literature) are held at the Mandarin Training Centre, National Taiwan University, 162 Hoping East Road, Section 1, Taipei 106.

THAILAND

Language of tuition Thai.
Academic year June to March.
Best contacts for information

- Ministry of University Affairs, 328 Sri Ayudhya Road, Bangkok 10400.
- Royal Thai Embassy, 29/30 Queen's Gate, London SW7 5JB. Tel (01) 589 0173.

1st degree courses

Length Variable.

Contact Universities themselves:

Chiang Mai University, Huay Kaew Road Muang District, Chiang Mai Province.
Chulalongkorn University, Phya Thai Road, Bangkok 10500.
Prince of Songkla University, Rector's Office, Hatyai Campus, 90110.
Ramkhamhaeng University, Huamark Bangkapi, Bangkok 10240.
Sri Nakharinwirot University, Soi 23 Sukumvit Road, Bangkok 11.
Sukhothair Thammathirat Open University, Office of University Affairs, Si Ayutthaya Road, Bangkok.

Entrance requirements
Completed secondary education and proficiency in Thai.

Grants
Some Thai Government Scholarships may be available to UK undergraduates with knowledge of Thai. Apply to Thailand National Commission for UNESCO, Ministry of Foreign Affairs, Bangkok.

Postgraduate

Contact As above.

Entrance requirements
Bachelor's degree. Knowledge of Thai not necessarily essential.

Grants
Thai Government Fellowships. Apply to Thailand National Commission for UNESCO, as above.

Language courses
Instruction in Thai for English speakers is available at:

Union Language School, 197/1 Silom Road, Bangkok.
AUA Language Center, 179 Rajdamri Road, Bangkok.

Other useful addresses
Thailand Tourist Information Office, 49 Albemarle Street,.
London W1. Tel (01) 499 7679.

TOGO

Language of tuition French.
Academic year September to July.
Best contacts for information
- University of Benin, PO Box 1515, Lomé.
- Embassy of Togo, 30 Sloane Street, London SW1. Tel (01) 235 0147-9.

Language courses
Courses in French as a foreign language are run each year by the Centre International de Recherche et d'Étude de Langues, Village du Bénin, PO Box 3724, Lomé.

TUNISIA

Best areas of study Arabic.
Language of tuition French. Arabic also preferred, but only necessary in certain faculties.
Academic year October to June.
Best contacts for information
- Office National des Oeuvres Universitaires (ONOU), 57 rue de Palestine, Tunis.
- Tunisian Embassy, 29 Prince's Gate, London SW7 1QG. Tel (01) 584 8117.

Language courses
The Institut Bourguiba des Langues Vivantes, 47 Avenue de la Liberté, 1002 Tunis Belvédère, runs a six week course in Arabic as a foreign language over the summer, and also a year long course lasting the whole academic year. Scholarships are also available; enquire at the same address.

Useful addresses
Tunisian National Tourist Office, 7a Stafford Street, London W1.

Tel (01) 499 2234.

Student travel
SOTUTOUR, 2 rue de Sparte, Tunis.

URUGUAY

Language of tuition Spanish.
Academic year March to November.
Best contacts for information
- Ministerio de Educación y Cultura, Serandi 444, Montevideo.
- Uruguayan Embassy, 48 Lennox Gardens, London SW1X 0DL. Tel (01) 589 8835.

VENEZUELA

Language of tuition Spanish.
Academic year September to July.
Best contacts for information
- Ministerio de Educación (EDUPLAN), edificio Esmeralda, Avda Los Próceres San Bernardino, Caracas.
- Venezuelan Embassy, 1 Cromwell Road, London SW7. Tel (01) 584 4206.

Student travel
Ontej, 2A Trans Campo Alegre, Cruce con Avda Fco de Miranda, Torre Ordival, Piso 12, PO Box 17696, Caracas.

VIETNAM

Embassy of the Socialist Republic of Vietnam, 12-14 Victoria Road, London W8. Tel (01) 937 1912.

ZAIRE

Language of tuition French.
Academic year October to June.
Best contacts for information
- Service des Oeuvres Estudiantines et Secteur de Cités Universitaries à la Université Nationale du Zaire, PO Box 13399,

Kinshasa 1.
● Embassy of the Republic of Zaire, 26 Chesham Place, London SW1X 8HH. Tel (01) 235 6137.

Useful Addresses

Association of Commonwealth Universities
36 Gordon Square
London WC1H 0PF
Tel (01) 387 8572

British Council
10 Spring Gardens
London SW1A 2BN
Tel (01) 930 8466

and
65 Davies Street
London W1Y 2AA
Tel (01) 499 8011

Central Bureau for Educational Visits & Exchanges
Seymour Mews House
Seymour Mews
London W1H 9PE
Tel (01) 486 5101

and
3 Bruntsfield Crescent
Edinburgh EH10 4HD
Tel (031) 447 8024

16 Malone Road
Belfast BT9 5BN
Tel (0232) 664418/9

Centre for Information on Language Teaching & Research (CILT)
Regents College
Inner Circle
Regents Park
London NW1 4NS
Tel (01) 486 8221

Commission of the European Communities
200 rue de la Loi
1049 Brussels
Belgium
Tel (010 322) 235 1111

Commission of the European Communities (London office)
8 Storeys Gate
London SW1
Tel (01) 222 8122

Department of Education and Science (England and Wales)
Elizabeth House
York Road
London SE1 7PH
Tel (01) 934 9000

Department of Education and Science for N. Ireland
Rathgael House
Balloo Road
Bangor
Co. Down BT19 2PR
Tel (0247) 466 311

Erasmus Bureau
15 rue d'Arlon
1040 Brussels
Belgium

Gabbitas, Truman and Thring
6-7-8 Sackville Street
London W1X 2BR
Tel (01) 734 0161

International Baccalaureate London Office
18 Woburn Square
London WC1H 0NS
Tel (01) 637 1682

International Bureau of Education (UNESCO)
PO Box 199
1211 Geneva 20

Switzerland
Tel (010 4122) 981 455

Scottish Education Dept
New St Andrew's House
St James Centre
Edinburgh EH1 3SY
Tel (031) 556 8400

UNESCO
7 place de Fontenoy
75700 Paris
France
Tel (010 33) 4568 1000

Further Reading

Directory of Work & Study in Developing Countries, David Leppard (Vacation Work, 1986)

Higher Education in the European Community, student edition (Commission of the European Communities, 1988; available from HMSO bookshops)

Home from Home (Central Bureau, 1987)

How to Get a Job Abroad, Roger Jones (Northcote House, 1989)

How to Live & Work in America, Steve Mills (Northcote House, 1988)

How to Live & Work in Australia, 2nd edition, Laura Veltman (Northcote House, 1990)

How to Live & Work in France, Nicole Prevost Logan (Northcote House, 1990).

How to Study & Live in Britain, Jane Woolfenden (Northcote House, 1990)

How to Teach Abroad, Roger Jones (Northcote House, 1989)

Scholarships Abroad, British Council (available from HMSO bookshops, annual)

Study Abroad (UNESCO)

Study Holidays (Central Bureau)

Studying & Living in Britain, British Council (Northcote House, 1990)

Time Off in Spain and Portugal, Teresa Tinsley (Horizon Books, 1989)

Working Abroad, Harry Brown (Northcote House, 1987)

Index